About
Clifton-upon-Teme
2000

Edited by Jerry Johns

CROWN HOUSE PRESS

ISBN 0 9535099 1 5

Published by the Crown House Press
Clifton-upon-Teme, Worcestershire WR6 6EN
crown.house@virgin.net

Printed by Axiom Design & Print
Bromsgrove, Worcestershire B60 3DR
Design/Layout by J. Mackay

CONTENTS

Acknowledgements

Editor: Jerry Johns

Editorial consultants: Cliff Barnard, June Haywood, Les Haywood

Contributors: Rosemary Collie, Jenny Farmer, June and Phil Haywood
                                 Keith Jaffrey, Bernard Pound

Photographs: Richard Bedhall, June Haywood, Chris Hurley, Jerry Johns
                                 Bernard Lewis, Bernard Pound, Pam Wojceichowski

Project Team: June Haywood, Richard Bedhall, Rosemary Collie,
                                 Bunty Crump, Michael Earthey, Jenny Farmer, Chris Hurley
                                 Jerry Johns, Bernard Lewis, Avis Owen, Joe Taylor
                                 Pam Wojceichowski

Funding sources: Teme Valley LEADER II
                                 Millennium Festival Awards For All
                                 Southern Marches Partnership
                                 The New Horizons Trust
                                 Herefordshire Community Regeneration Scheme

Donations: Clifton Gardeners
                                 Janet Morley (New Inn)
                                 Heather Hurley
                                 Barbara Williams

Foreword

This book would not have been possible without the assistance and co-operation of an enormous number of people, too many to list here though their names doubtless appear somewhere within these pages.

When it was first suggested that we produce a book about our village to mark the Millennium, I don't think any of us imagined just what an enormous undertaking it would be. Raising the money in itself proved a daunting task, but we were fortunate in obtaining generous grants from several local bodies in addition to our own fund-raising efforts.

From the start, however, we were determined that this would be a book about the village as it was at the beginning of this year, viewed across the year that has just passed. We wanted as many people as possible living in the village and neighbourhood to be included and involved and the response has been magnificent. The project team spent many hours and weeks contacting every household, gathering information, researching and checking facts and taking photographs. The result is an extraordinary collaborative production which truly reflects Clifton-upon-Teme as it was at the turn of the millennium and one, I think you will agree, that provides a fascinating record of our village community which I hope will continue to delight future generations. We have certainly enjoyed producing it.

June Haywood
Project Team Leader
April 2000

The About Clifton-upon-Teme 2000 book project team:
(Standing, left to right)
Chris Hurley, Bernie Lewis,
Mike Earthey, Joe Taylor,
Rosemary Collie, Jerry Johns,
Richard Bedhall.
(Seated) Bunty Crump,
Jenny Farmer, June Haywood,
Pam Wojciechowski, Avis Owen.

Clifton-upon-Teme and Sapey Common:
Reproduced from the 1999 Explorer 204 1:25,000 map by permission of Ordnance
Survey on behalf of The Controller of Her Majesty's Stationery Office, (c) Crown copyright MC 1000311475

Introduction

About Clifton-upon-Teme 2000 is the story of an ancient Worcestershire village at the turn of the millennium. It embraces the parish of Clifton-upon-Teme, nearby Sapey Common as well as local farms and homesteads in the area and is essentially a product of the people who live there; their lives, their occupations and local activities throughout 1999.

What emerges from the pages of this book is a portrait of a truly remarkable community at the dawn of the 21st century. A community of young and old, newcomers and lifelong residents, living together in one of the most beautiful parts of Britain.

Clifton-upon-Teme 1999

Much of the social life of the village centres round the three principal institutions, church, school and the two local inns, though the shop and the post office play their part too.

Clifton-upon-Teme 1900

Clifton, a village as old as the past millennium itself, has a strong sense of community spirit. It has been fortunate in retaining many of the services and amenities that other communities elsewhere have lost: school, bus service, post office, shop, surgery, garage, pubs, recreation ground, church and many clubs and organisations. From the cradle to the grave, there are amenities and support services for all ages: a toddler group and under-5s nursery, through school and church, tennis club and pony club, gardeners and ramblers to the Bowls Club and Friendship Club - there is something for almost every age and interest.

Farming continues to dominate the life and economy of Clifton as it has done for generations, even though 1999 saw it going through one of the most economically depressed periods in living memory. But there are encouraging signs of new enterprise taking root in the area, linked to the information technology revolution. Buildings that once served an agricultural purpose now house occupants whose business depends on connection to the Internet. Ancient and modern technologies existing side by side.

About Clifton-upon-Teme 2000 is a snapshot of a rural community at a particular moment in time, but one which will serve as enduring record for future generations, just as the 11th century Domesday survey has in the past.

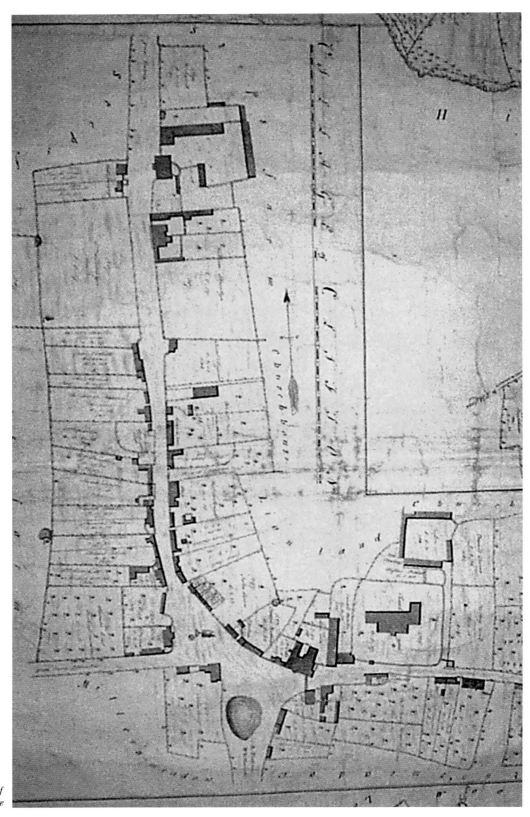

*1819 map of
Clifton village*

History

Although there is evidence of Roman occupation in the area around Clifton-upon-Teme, the village is considered an excellent example of an Anglo-Saxon settlement situated some 600 feet up overlooking the River Teme along the ancient salt route that led from Droitwich to Leominster.

The early inhabitants practised crop rotation on a communal system, using oxen to plough the land. Villagers let their pigs forage for food in Clifton Wood and gathered honey from local bees.

The earliest surviving mention of the village is in the Latin charter of King Athelstan granting it to the monks of St Peter's Monastery at Worcester in 934 AD when it is referred to as Clistun ultra Tame.

During the time of the wars with the Welsh, the Manor of Clifton became established and was granted Royal Borough status by Henry III in 1270, allowing it to hold a weekly market on Thursdays and an annual four-day fair. The original manor house, built around 1200 on the site of the present Lion Inn, eventually came to be used as a hostelry for travellers en route between Worcester and Tenbury Wells.

Village children outside St. Kenelm's Church c1900

There is mention of a priest in Clifton at the time of the Domesday survey. The church of St. Kenelm, one of only eight named after the Saxon boy King of Mercia murdered on the Clent Hills, dates back to the 13th century. In the south aisle is an effigy of Sir Ralph de Wysham, a crusader knight whose son built Woodmanton Manor in 1325. The church spire was rebuilt in the 17th century after being blown down, and was struck by lightning in 1884 when it was replaced by the present wooden spire. Over the doorway inside hangs a Royal Achievement indicating that Clifton was once a Royal Borough.

The manor of Clifton passed to the Winnington family of Stanford Court in the 18th century, and the village remained part of Stanford Court Estate until 1932 when most of the houses and farms were sold by auction when part of the estate was put up for sale.

The Winnington family have lived in Worcestershire since the 17th century, inheriting the manors of Clifton and Homme Castle. The first baronetcy was bestowed in 1775, with the original family seat at Stanford Court overlooking the Teme Valley at Stanford Bridge. The building was severely damaged by fire in 1882. The family sold Stanford Court in 1949, moving to Brockhill Court three miles away until December 1999 when the present baronet, 92-year-old Sir Francis Winnington, and his wife announced they would be moving to their London home. Educated at Eton, Sir Francis Winnington joined the Army in 1931, was captured by enemy forces at Dunkirk in 1940 and was a prisoner until his release in 1943. He married in 1944 and he and Lady Winnington have a daughter, Charmian.

Clifton-upon-Teme 1855

Nearly 150 years ago, the population of the village was a little over 500, not far below its present-day total. The village school thrived with around 75 pupils under the care of the headmaster, Frederick James Noad. He was a remarkably active member of the community, for in addition to his role as schoolmaster, he was postmaster (collections at 4pm daily and 10.30am on Sundays), church organist and collector of premiums for the Hope Mutual Life Assurance Society. His wife Lucy also taught at the school as well as caring for her infant daughter Fanny.

Village life in 1855 centred on the church. The Rev. Slade Baker had only recently arrived at the Vicarage, his predecessor having moved to the Isle of Wight to become chaplain to Queen Victoria. A little while later the Rev. Baker, at the age of 30, married a girl ten years younger than himself.

After the church and the school, the next most important buildings in Clifton at that time were the three inns, the Lion, the Unicorn and the Crown. The landlord of the first, known then as the Red Lion, was 33-year-old Joe Derbyshire who made a living from selling beer, taking in lodgers and farming a few acres nearby. The Unicorn at the other end of the village was owned by local farmer, butcher and victualler, John Horton. The Crown on the other hand was run by widow Hannah Hodges and her son Joseph who was to take it over following after his mother's death a few years later. By 1880 both the Unicorn and the Crown had ceased to sell beer, while halfway down Clifton hill an ale and cider house known as Shortlands run by the Griffiths family was eventually to become what is now the New Inn.

Evidence of Clifton's self-sufficiency can be seen in the wide range of trades and skills that existed among its inhabitants at the time. Michael Potterran a tailor's shop. William Rowley and his wife Mary traded from premises now occupied by Clifton Stores as a grocer, draper and shoemaker, while further down the street young Frederick Williams had also set up shop as a general dealer, grocer and draper.

The old forge, 1965

As well as the village blacksmith's shop run by Thomas Jones, another run by Edward Roberts and his sons Edwin and Shadrack carried on a steady trade from their smithy. Both blacksmiths continued well into the 1880s by which time Shadrack had taken over his father's business and had a virtual monopoly in the parish.

Law and order was firmly in the custody of police constable James Dovey. There was a wheelwright, a saddle maker, a miller, several dressmakers and enough business in the area to keep Richard Arminger employed as a castrator well into his eighties! And no doubt Joe Lipscombe's bus to Worcester was better patronised than the present day service.

At the time of the 1881 census, many of the residents of the parish were employed in agricultural occupations.

1881 Census - Clifton-upon-Teme
Occupations given

Agricultural labourers	40	Horse breakers	2
Baker	1	House painter	1
Blacksmiths	6	Innkeepers	2
Bootmaker	1	Laundresses	3
Bricklayer/Building labourers	7	Machinists	2
Building contractor	1	Miller	1
Butchers	2	Nurse	2
Carpenters	5	Police officer	1
Clerk in Holy Orders	1	Schoolmaster/Teachers	3
Commission agent	1	Seamstresses	2
Draper	1	Shirtmaker	1
Dressmaker	1	Tailors	4
Farmers	16	Vet/castrator	1
Farm servants	16	Wheelwright	1
General/Domestic servants	15	Wood sawyer	1
General labourers	24		
Grocer	1		
Groom	1	TOTAL	167

Today, the population has increased to a little over 600, largely due to the addition of 90 new houses in the 1960s in Kenelm Road, Manor Road and Saxon Close, and more recently in Forge Meadows. There is still the church, a primary school, general stores, a post office and the two inns in addition to the village hall, a garage and a doctors' surgery.

The village itself lies on B4204 road that leads westward from Worcester to Tenbury Wells. Leading off the main road is the Whitbourne road and Hope Lane. Heading northwest from the village, the main road crosses the county boundary between Worcestershire and Herefordshire, then passes through Sapey Common to Upper Sapey. Branching off the main road through Sapey Common is Cliftonswood Lane, leading to Cliftonswood Farm; Rock Lane, leading down to Southstone Rock, once the site of a hermitage where travelling monks would seek shelter in the caves; and Park Lane.

c1914

1999

20th Century Clifton-upon-Teme: the last 100 years

At the beginning of the last century, the population of Clifton-upon-Teme stood at around 500. Most of the properties in the village itself belonged to the Stanford Court Estate.

Kelly's Directory 1900
Clifton-on-Teme

David Davis, Copperfields
Rev. Robert George Griffiths MA, vicar, Vicarage
Emmie Betley and Miss Florence Wincoops, private school, Bayton Villa
Charles Edward Boddington, farmer, Ham Castle
Jarvis Markman Clayton, Red Lion
Charles Cooper, farmer and hop grower, The Noak
Mrs Jane Davis, shopkeeper
Edward Dorrell, farmer and hop grower, Church Farm
Richard Depper, farmer, Woodmanton
David Evans, farmer, Ayngstree
Miss Charlotte Farmer, farmer, Pitlands
Philip Farmer, farmer and hop grower, The Steps
Fred Hall, grocer and draper, Post Office
Ernest Haywood, carpenter and blacksmith
Thomas Hill, builder and carrier, Mount Pleasant
John Jauncey, farmer, Moorfields
Evan Jones, farmer, Salford Farm
William Jones, tailor
Leslie Legge, miller (water), Ham Mill
George Lewis, carpenter, parish clerk
Thomas Lewis, farmer and miller (water), Holland Mill
William Martin, New Inn and farmer
Robert Matthews, shoemaker
Shadrach Roberts, blacksmith
Robert Farquhar Rogers, clerk to Parish Council
John Spilsbury, farmer and hop grower, The Hope
John and William Wainwright, machinists
William Warren, farmer
Frederick Warren, butcher
Samuel Weaver, surveyor, house agent
Richard and Thomas Yapp, farmers, Ham Farm
George Yarnold, farmer, Clifton Wood
Henry and Mrs Brown, headmaster and mistress

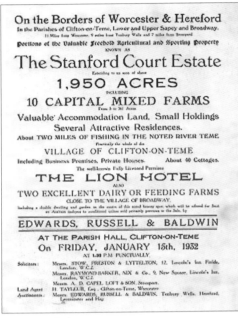

*Sale of Stanford
Court Estate 1932*

1903

The first mains water supply, pumped up from the pump house at Holloway Brook at the bottom of Hope Lane, is connected to Clifton via the reservoir in the field behind Chapel House. Five water taps are installed along the main street through the village (one of which survives on the Green opposite the Lion Inn).

1914

St. Kenelm's Church bells are re-hung in July and a Treble bell, a gift from Sir Francis Winnington, the 5th baronet, added in memory of Sir Francis's son who died in 1913 at the age of 31.

1922

The Clifton-upon-Teme Memorial Hall officially opened, having been built by public subscription in memory to local men killed in the 1st World War. The first Council houses are built in Hope Lane and in the Old Road.

1932

Part of the Stanford Court Estate is sold by auction in the Memorial Hall at Clifton on 15th January. Nearly 60 lots, including most of the properties in the village, many bought by their tenants.

1934

Fred Hall, owner of the village shop, and his son Roy are killed in a flying accident near Cirencester on Saturday, 13th January. The tragedy is all the more shocking because few people knew he even had a pilot's licence. Electricity comes to Clifton.

*Berrows
Worcester
Journal,
January 1934*

BERROW'S WORCESTER JOURNAL   Saturday, January 20 19

PLANE CRASH NEAR CIRENCESTER

CLIFTON-ON-TEME'S LOSS

Mr. R.F.Hall and Son Killed

News was received in Worcester on Saturday evening that Mr Fred Rowland Hall of Clifton-on-Teme, and his son Roy, had been killed in an aeroplane accident at Sapperton, near Cirencester. The accident occurred in the afternoon, but for a time there was some doubt about the identity of the persons in the aeroplane because, on the remains of a driving licence, the name and address was deciphered as Rowlands, Clevedon, near Worcester. But ultimately reference was made to the Cotswold Aero Club, Gloucester, and identity was established. Mr Hall and his son left their home at Clifton on Saturday morning, going away by car, and it is now known that Mr Hall (who was a member of the Cotswold Aero Club) and his son took off from the club's aerodrome at about 11 o'clock. An hour later they had crashed, and their machine had burned itself out.

acquired his business premises number of other properties in the and its environs. He was of a nature and well versed in for him, and in games tennis was recreation. But he was mechanic and his advice was sought and services were readily his neighbours when demanded. Mr Hall was churchman and was identified with parochial org He served about two churchwarden at the parish had acted as Hon. Secretary Parochial Church Council for longer period. He was a member Committee of Management of the Hall, and he showed a keen int welfare of the Tennis Club, he was Hon. Secretary. Roy

*Fred and Roy Hall
outside Hall's Stores*

1939
The first child evacuees arrive in Clifton from London.

1943
PoW camp located at Blue Shot in Pound Lane.

1944
RAF Blenheim bomber lands in a field near Salford Court

1946
First Council houses built in Manor Road.

1961
Mains water arrives in Clifton, replacing the Holloway Brook supply via the reservoir.

Clifton-upon-Teme 1967

1967
Saxon Close development begins and more houses built in Manor Road.

1970
Kenelm Close development

1977
Village pageant staged in July at Woodmanton, celebrating 700 years of Clifton history.

1996
Forge Meadows development completed.

Memories of the 20th Century

Peggy Hooper recalls the post war years in Clifton when her family then lived at Old Unicorn Cottage.

"During the long summer holidays from school, we worked out in the fields with my mother, pea-picking and hop-picking, sometimes to help pay for the Doctor's bill from the previous winter. One Sunday during the summer we would pile into Dad's Austin Seven and drive to Weston-super-Mare for the day. We would all sit on the beach while Mum cut up a loaf of bread and gave us slices with home-made butter and strawberry jam. I still can't think how we all got into that little car.

"When I was in my teens, I would go with my mother to the women's club on Monday nights in the village hall. On Tuesday nights we had a film show, on Wednesday nights it was youth club and on Friday night we had a whist drive or a dance."

* * *

Herbert Yeomans (1915-1996) lived at Homme Castle from 1927 until the outbreak of war in 1939 and later wrote about life at that time:

"I well recall those September mornings with a light mist and little bit chilly before the sun broke through, the hop pickers would kindle a wood fire and frizzle bacon on the end of a stick. How good it tasted and smelt in the open air. That type of September morning is still referred to in this area as a 'hop picking morning'. On Saturday night a lot of the pickers would gather at the New Inn in Clifton, usually consuming more beer than they could carry. They would roll back down the hill to Homme Castle singing lustily, normally going off to sleep quickly on reaching their billets.

"We killed our pigs for the house sometime between November and February. Our local pig butcher was Harry Webb from Clifton who would walk with his pig killing tackle

down through Clifton parks to Homme Castle, never taking up the offer of being collected in our car. He was a lean, active man, and was also a sheep shearer, always using a pair of well sharpened shears, scorning the more modern shearing machines. He was reputed to have walked from Clifton to the three counties show at Hereford, won first prize for shearing and walked back."

John Mann at Pitlands Farm recalls that his father, Sydney, owned one of the first lorries in the area, operated with only one forward and one reverse gear. "He did some haulage for neighbours, and was also 'undertaker's mate' to the local undertaker, Ernest Haywood, but after some pretty hair-raising experiences he decided to give this up, deciding it was not for him. Farm work was then the leading industry, and father used to rent other orchards in the area, offering employment to local families, many of whom still live in the village.

Pitlands Farm

"During the war years, the horse that pulled the village fire engine was kept here at Pitlands. I imagine the fires would have been quite big by the time someone had come from the village, caught the horse and taken it back to harness it to the appliance in Clifton.

Ken Harris, a wartime evacuee from London at the age of eight who spent two years at Church House Farm remembers the ring of sandbags built round the big tree that then stood on the village green. "It would probably have been a machine gun post in the event of this country being invaded but fortunately was only used as a refuge for the infants class during air raid practices. For these, the Headmaster Mr Carter would blow a whistle and everybody had to grab their gasmask and evacuate the school. The infants would run across the green and crouch inside the sandbagged wall while the junior and senior classes had to run down the Whitbourne Road to the field on the first bend where they were expected to lay flat on the ground and as near to the hedge as possible until told the practice was over.

Clifton Home Guard platoon outside the Lion Hotel.
Denny Lippit is second from the right in the middle row.

"While playing on the village green during a school break one day, a very low flying aeroplane passed right over the school. It was so low that we could see the pilot and some of his crew and waved to them. I can remember thinking that it was strange that it had black crosses under its wings and I decided it must have been an ambulance plane and its red crosses had been painted black because of the war. It was only later we found out that it was a German bomber on its way to machine gun an army barracks somewhere near Tenbury."

Denny Lippit, now aged 82 having worked at Salford Court farm for 60 years, remembers the evening an RAF Blenheim bomber landed in a field near the farm in May 1944. The aircraft had lost its way in fog en route to Market Drayton. One of the men on board, Wing Commander Bob Danby, wanted to know where the nearest barber was so that he could get his moustache trimmed. When word reached the village, the children came to look and the local Home Guard stood guard for a short time until they were replaced by a military detachment. The task of removing the aircraft from the muddy field involved removing the wings and dragging the fuselage to the road with tractors where it was loaded onto a low-loader (through the gate at the entrance to the field opposite Otheridge Pool Cottage). The low-loader was itself in trouble at Ham Bridge because its load was too wide and a crane had to be sent for before it could continue the journey to Worcester.

Phil Haywood recalls some of the severe winters of years past in Clifton.
"Snow would be driven by the wind up into the roof space in some of the older houses and had to be cleared before it melted and brought the ceilings down. On one occasion, 140 buckets of snow were cleared from under the rafters of Forge House.

"In 1947 the snow was so deep that a grocery van was stuck for six weeks along the road approaching the village at the top of Clifton hill. Snow filled the roads so that it was possible to walk above the hedges, with only the telegraph poles to guide by. Flour was brought up to the bakery on a sledge, pulled by horses across the fields, while farmers took milk to collection points by the same route. The village school was closed for much of the time between the end of January until April while the snow remained, and going to school in Worcester was out of the question."

1999 - A Year in the Life of Clifton-upon-Teme

January

The Clifton Millennium Book project team meets for the first time.

March

Renovation work on the BP hut is celebrated by the Guides, Brownies & Rainbows. Fauré's Requiem is performed by an augmented St Kenelm's choir.

April

A public meeting to discuss the Millennium Book Project is held in the Village Hall, attended by Grenville Sheringham of Team Leader II. The Annual Parish Church meeting is also held at the Village Hall.

May

The Clifton-on-Teme Primary School May Fayre is held on the village green. The Clifton Bowling Club hold an open evening. A Spring Sale in aid of Christian Aid is held at the Village Hall.

Floodwater on Clifton Hill, April 1999

July

The Millennium Book Project draw takes place at the Lion Inn. The Clifton Gardeners annual Open Gardens day attracts large numbers of visitors to gardens throughout the village. The St. Kenelm's Church bells are rung following their return to the belfry. A progressive supper is held to raise funds for the Millennium Book Project. The annual Pet's Service takes place at St Kenelm's Church.

Sheila Burgoyne, June Haywood, Sue Palmer and Peggy Hooper at the Open Gardens day, July 1999

August

The St Kenelm's Classic & Custom Motorcycle Show is held at the Village Hall, opened by the Rev. Lionel Fanthorpe. Several local residents take part in a sponsored walk to raise funds for the Millennium Book Project. The total eclipse of the sun is watched by villagers on the green.

September
A weekend Flower Festival is held at St Kenelm's Church depicting 'Clifton Village Life'. A special service to dedicate the refurbished bells is held on the Sunday.

October
Harvest Festival is celebrated at Clifton-upon-Teme Primary School. A Black Country evening is held in the Village Hall by the Clifton Bowling Club.

November
A Sound & Light Show takes place at the Village Hall. The annual Royal British Legion parade and service is held at St Kenelm's church.

December
New Year's Eve celebrations are held on the village green at midnight.

Flower Festival, St. Kenelm's Church

Christmas lights outside Bury's Place

St. Kenelm's Parish Church

There has probably been a church building in Clifton for over a thousand years. According to legend, the murder of Kenelm, boy Prince of Mercia, took place in 819 AD and it would have been unlikely that a dedication to Kenelm would have been made without a Christian building of some kind in the village. The present building was commenced around 1200 and the Woodmanton chapel added in 1350, so what is seen today is that which has stood for almost 800 years. The spire was rebuilt in the 17th century after being blown down, only to be struck by lightning in June, 1884.

The stained glass east window was erected in 1882 by the Rev. Robert Moncrieff, vicar 1875-85. In June 1897, the clock was added to the tower to commemorate the 60th year of Queen Victoria's reign. The oak altar, reredos and side panels were presented by Lady Winnington in 1932 in memory of her husband Sir Francis, the 5th baronet, who had died the previous year. The oak choir stalls were installed in 1934 in memory of Fred Hall, who had kept the village stores, and his son Roy.

Today the village still has its resident priest, the Reverend Clifford Owen. He is also Rector of the neighbouring communities of the Shelsleys and Lower Sapey. In addition, he acts as the Ecumenical Officer for Worcestershire, a job which not only takes him around the county but beyond it. In reality, he gives about a quarter of his time to Clifton, but as in most modern parishes, the Rector is supported by a team carrying out the pastoral, teaching and administrative work, comprising six church wardens and three lay-readers with two others in training. Although the ancient office of churchwarden still exists, present day churchwardens carry a large pastoral and organisational load.

Rev. Clifford Owen outside St. Kenelm's church.

Throughout the life of St. Kenelm's church, says Clifford Owen, Christian worship would have taken place without a break at least weekly on the site. "If only those stones could speak and tell us what they have seen and heard these last eight centuries! As the year turns to 2000, Christians still gather to worship God in Clifton. Every week about 50 different people attend worship, about 100 monthly and at festivals around 150. Add to that the numbers attending for the special occasions of life and over the course of a year about 30 per cent of the village population will enter this historic place of worship."

St. Kenelm's church choir.

As the clock neared midnight on New Year's Eve, people gathered in St. Kenelm's church to spend some time in quiet before processing to the village green with candles to herald the new millennium. "They were remembering that the founder of Christianity was born 2000 years ago and His influence still persists in this remote but beautiful part of rural England," he adds.

Rectors of St. Kenelm's Church

1304	Simon de Bedeston	
	Nicholas de la Hulle	
1361	John Scodiar	
1369	William Weston	
1370	William Pengre	
	William Pennkryche	
	Richard Feryngale	
1406	William Lorymer	
1408	John Cleve	
1409	William Overton	
1410	William Spark	
	Richard Henthale	
1418	John Noxton	
	Thomas Combey	
1443	Henry Martley	
1445	John Monk	
	William Yates	
1489	John Bracy	
	John Wolfe	
1533	Edward Wright	
1546	William Callowshill	
1556	Robert Barret	
1562	William Perkyns	
1565	Arthur Hewett	
	Gabriel Cliffe	
1598	William Leigh	✠
1607	Richard Nurse	✠
1638	Roland Crosby MA	
1643	John Greene	
	Samuel Tiler	
1658	John Barbour MA	✠
1686	Acton Cremer MA	✠

1689	William Johnson DD	
1698	Edmund Weaver MA	
1700	John Stanley BA	✠
1707	Thomas Woodhouse BA	✠
1741	Thomas King MA	
1771	George Butt DD	
1787	Thomas Cookes	
1804	Denham James J. Cookes MA	
1809	Edward Winnington Ingram MA	
1817	Charles Fox Winnington BA	
1841	John Pearson MA	
1843	Arthur H. Winnington Ingram MA	
1845	George Prothero MA	
1853	Slade Baker MA	
1875	Robert Chichester Moncrieff BA	
1885	Martin Brereton Buckle	
1895	John Stroud Maber	✠
1899	Robert George Griffiths MA	
1927	Charles Hodgetts Bagott MA	✠
1931	William Irwin Crump	
1944	John Leslie Norden	
1951	Edward Somerville Collie MA	
1957	Thomas Claud Leonard Vincent MA	
1965	John Alexander Harper	
1972	Donald Heggie	✠
1979	Alan Robert Archer	
1981	Patrick John Bogan Hobson MC	
1989	Philip Clifford Owen	

✠ *Buried at Clifton-upon-Teme*

St Kenelm's Church Bells

Peter Pheysey lowers one of the bells in the church tower

The highlight of the year for the eight members of the St Kenelm's Church bell ringing team was ringing the bells in peal on the afternoon of Thursday, 15th July for the first time following the three day operation to re-hang them in the belfry on their return from the bell foundry in Loughborough where they had undergone restoration work since Easter.

Five of the bells had hung in the belfry since 1668 - the sixth treble bell was presented in 1914 by Sir Francis Winnington when the peal was last rehung - until, on 15th April 1999, they were slowly lowered to the floor of the tower and manoeuvred through the church door. A team of local volunteers, including bell-ringers Bob Davis and Peter Pheysey, Colling Robson and the Diocesan Bells Advisor, David Beacham, who supervised the removal of the bells, was involved in stripping down and removing the six main bells and smaller Sanctus bell, cleaning the belfry, painting the bell-frame and re-hanging the six refurbished bells. The Sanctus bell was added later.

The re-hanging operation was assisted by Phil Haywood, who supervised the loading and unloading; David Yarnold who provided transport for the bells to and from Loughborough, and drivers Mike Lewis and Matthew Haywood. The bellhanger foreman took charge of the lifting operation to return the bells to the belfry in the church tower some 30 feet from the ground.

The original budgeted cost of the project had been nearly £25,000, but by doing much of the work themselves the team has reduced this to around £18,000, much of which was raised by donations from local residents. When the anticipated National Millennium Bells Fund grant was not forthcoming, project co-ordinator Bob Davis pressed on with both the project itself and the fund raising - a major challenge but one that was successfully overcome. The result, according to Bob who is also a member of the bell ringing team, is a peal of retuned bells which will be ringing for many years to come.

Clifton-upon-Teme bellringers

Once the bells had returned, the St Kenelm's Bell Ringers continued to meet as usual on Tuesday evenings for practice as well as on Sundays and the occasional Saturday wedding. They are members of the County Association of Bell Ringers, a local guild promoting the development of bell ringing. Captain of the St Kenelm's Bell Ringers, Richard Speed, is a representative member of the Central Council of Church Bell Ringers, the national body of ringers.

Parochial Church Council

The St. Kenelm's Parochial Church Council supports the work of the vicar and lay readers by helping to promote the pastoral, evangelistic and ecumenical mission of the church as well as maintain the fabric of the building itself.

The six meetings of the PCC in 1999 were dominated by financial issues, including fund raising for specific projects such as the restoration of the church bells, or meeting the parish's annual quota obligation. There are four sub-committees reporting to the PCC: a standing committee; a fabric committee responsible for small maintenance work and advising on larger repairs that are necessary; a children in church committee planning monthly family services; and a bell restoration committee overseeing the restoration of the bells.

The PCC's fund raising activities during 1999 included the Classic Bike Show in August.

St. Kenelm's Parochial Church Council:

Incumbent:	Rev. Clifford Owen
Reader:	Ted Farrell
Churchwardens:	Patricia Collett, Mike Snelling
Deanery Synod Representatives:	Brian Hoare, Pat Snelling
Elected Representatives:	Pippa Balch, Hilary Bloomer, Michael Brookes, Brian Hoare, Dorothy Leavey (Organist & Choir-mistress), Angela Niblett, Peter Pheysey, Avis Owen, Douglas Ratcliffe, Anne Speed (Treasurer), Richard Speed

The St. Kenelm's Parochial Church Council

Clifton-upon-Teme Primary School

The original school building in the village dates from 1844 and housed the National School 'for the education of the children of the parishes of Clifton and Sapey Pritchard', supported by voluntary contributions and subject to both diocesan and government inspection. In 1855 it had 75 pupils in the care of the headmaster, Frederick James Noad, and his wife Lucy. In addition to his educational duties, Mr Noad was also the village postmaster, organist and agent for the Hope Mutual Life Assurance Society. A School Board of five members was formed in 1883, and by 1896, Henry West and his wife Emily had succeeded as headmaster and mistress in charge of 60 boys and girls and 40 infants.

Pupils and staff outside Clifton-upon-Teme School 1908

Mr George Carter, appointed headteacher in the 1920s, retired in 1955 and was succeeded by Ray Leech, followed by Gerry Gautrey in 1960, Ken Davies in 1965, Cecil Drew in 1969 and Ron Maddocks in 1974 until 1994 when the present head, Debbie Mitchell was appointed.

The school celebrated its 150th anniversary in 1994.

*Village schoolchildren
dancing round the
maypole on the green,
1999*

At the end of 1999, 58 pupils attended Clifton-upon-Teme Primary School, aged from four to 11 years of age, arranged in three classes. During the year, the children had all participated in the design and making of three rag rugs, with a fourth completed by parents, featuring the four elements: earth, fire, air and water. In addition, the PTA raised money to present each child with a commemorative millennium plate.

In addition to Debbie Mitchell, head-teacher for six years, there are two other full-time teaching members of staff, Sarah Wilkins and Karen Driver, and a part-time teacher, Bob Percival. School secretary Brigette Manton took over in 1998 from her mother, Bunty Crump, who retired after 25 years. Other members of staff include lunchtime supervisors Daphne Robson and Sue Williams who, with Sally Wakefield, also assists in the classroom; and caretaker Margaret Butler.

Head-teacher Debbie Mitchell said: "We are proud to be a small school. We believe that all the children are entitled to enjoy their time here in an environment where they can feel happy and secure. We aim to provide a caring family atmosphere and work in partnership with parents and the village community."

Class 1, Christmas 1999

Clifton-upon-Teme Primary School, January 2000

Class 1
Ben Atkinson, Abigail Birks, Paul Bullock, Roxanne Bullock, Jack Butler, Lydia Cahill, Georgina Dennis, Amelia Flower, Christopher Card, Rhiannon Cole, Tom Crump, Lucinda Haywood, Naomi Higton, Jessica McLaren, Matthew Morley, Verity Richards, Morgan Smart, Abigail Smith, Ellena Smith, Kate Smith, Brett Thompson, Jacob Wadley.

Class 2
Sam Atkinson, Carly Bullock, Adam Cale, Jodie Card, Stella Card, Gemma Davies, William Diment, Esther Higton, Oliver Hotchkiss, Jay Lawson-Pearce, Gina Mayfield, Philippa Redfern, Lydia Richards, Jonathan Verry, Connor Wadley, Jack Wickens.

Class 3
Amy Butler, Ben Cahill, Laurence Cole, Phoebe Cox, Shane Davis, Christopher Diment, Lauren Holloway, Andrew Mitchell Alexander Nuthall, Laura Richards, Thomas Richards, David Small, Madison Smart, Rebecca Smith, Tabitha Sparey, Richard Taylor, Zachary Thompson, Jessica Wadley, Alice Wakefield, Louise Wickens.

Pupils and staff outside Clifton-upon-Teme School 2000

School Governors

The ten governors who make up the school's governing body have close ties with the village. Pamela Wojciechowski, serving her first year as Chairman in 1999, dedicated herself to the well-being, happiness and education of all the pupils as well as the support of staff and parents. Vice-Chairman Chris Cale, a parent governor, spent much of his time carefully planning the school's budget. The two LEA-appointed governors were Bunty Crump, a former member of staff, and Pat Snelling who replaced Anne Speed during the year. Parent governors include Hilary Higton and Diane Richards, with two children at the school and involved with special needs of pupils.

Two co-opted governors were Roger Atkinson, involved with the school's building, health and safety issues, and Mark Fletcher, a former pupil involved also with health and safety issues. Head-teacher Debbie Mitchell and Sarah Wilkins, a member of the teaching staff, are also governors.

The Friends of Clifton-upon-Teme Primary School

The Friends of Clifton school are a group of hard-working parents, teachers and governors who organise fund-raising events in aid of the school. In 1999, the Friends committee consisted of Mandy Card, Heather Nuthall, Lorna Davies and Ann Cale. Between them, they organised a variety of events including the May Fayre, Christmas bazaar, car boot sale and a floral demonstration in addition to a monthly lottery. The proceeds have been used to purchase such items as tape recorders, dining room tables and a fridge freezer for the school as well as the special millennium plates issued to every child.

Schoolhouse Under 5s Nursery

The Schoolhouse Under 5s Nursery celebrated 21 years as the village pre-school group for children aged from two and a half years to rising five year olds. Open four mornings a week from 8.30am until midday, it is run by leader Jackie Gilbert, one of three local parents who founded the group in the village hall in 1978, and four other members of staff: Pat Stevenson, Nina Haines, Ann Goddard and Debbie Smith, with support from a committee of nine. During the year, a video was made of the children and screened at the open evening in October. In addition, parents and staff redecorated the room at the Schoolhouse behind the village green now occupied by the group.

Clifton-upon-Teme Toddler Group

The Clifton Toddler Group, led by two young village mothers, Hilary Higton and Nicola Clarke, meets every Wednesday morning in the school. It has over 30 children and babies registered with it, with around 15 coming each week accompanied by a parent or grandparent. The group has become a lively social occasion for both children and adults, with play activities, singing and drinks for all.

Clifton-on-Teme Parish Council

The first meeting of Clifton-on-Teme Parish Council took place on December 4th 1894. The Minute book recording that meeting survives:

In 1898, the Parish Council was concerned with such issues as the extension of the churchyard, the establishment of a Telegraph Office in the village and gates obstructing the Whitbourne lane.

More than 100 years later, the issues dominating the Parish Council's agenda in 1999 concerned a proposal for 'social housing development' in Hope Lane and a land-slip on Clifton Hill that had resulted in temporary traffic lights in use there for much of the year. Other perennial issues included the speed and parking of vehicles in the village, rubbish deposited around the skip and low water pressure in the village.

Parish Council Chairman Bernard Pound inspecting the roadworks on Clifton Hill

Parish Council Chairman, Bernard Pound - elected in April in succession to Douglas Ratcliffe - said there had been a number of objections both to the proposed development in Hope Lane and the Council's support for it. A special meeting of the Council discussed the matter in June but one member of the Council, Kate Harper, resigned in October. She was replaced by Colin Watmore.

"What strikes me most, as a comparatively new member of the Council, is how little notice most villagers take of our work until something like the proposed social housing grabs their attention," said Bernard.

Earlier in the year, shortly after the Council had discussed an application by the owner of a private airstrip at Hanley William to increase the number of permitted flying days, Phil Haywood also resigned from the Council after nearly 40 years as a member and former Chairman. The death of former Chairman Ernie Maudsley in December further reduced the Council to six members by the year end.

Clifton Parish Council (December 1999)

Clifton-upon-Teme Parish Council, December 1999: (Left to right)
Colin Watmore, Bert Bradley, Liz Peel (Clerk), Bernard Pound (Chairman), Barbara Wilday,
Barbara Williams (District Councillor), Douglas Ratcliffe, Dorothy Leavey.

Clubs and Organisations

Royal British Legion

The 30 members of the Clifton Men's branch of the Royal British Legion celebrated the millennium and the branch's long association with St. Kenelm's parish church by replacing the old flagpole in the churchyard with a new aluminium pole and Union Jack flag which flown for the first time on Armistice Day in November. Members also gave a St. George's flag to the PCC for use on religious festivals. The first British Legion branch in the village was formed after the 1st World War; after closing in 1967, it began again in 1982 and has since continued to meet quarterly in the Village Hall and again held its annual dinner in November at Sapey Golf Club.

The Women's branch of the British Legion in Clifton has 18 members, but has in fact been in existence longer than the men's branch, having breen chaired for over 30 years by Phil Haywood's mother Nellie who later became branch president. It continued to meet monthly during 1999, raising funds including the annual poppy appeal, but branch secretary Christine House admits: "we are having difficulty recruiting new members."

Tennis Club

The Clifton Tennis Club's 50 members were able to look back with well-deserved pride in 1999 on the 15 years since the Club was first formed in 1986. In the early days, members met at Martley to play until strenuous fund-raising efforts by the newly-formed Clifton Playing Fields Association led to two hard tennis court being built in the village in the autumn of 1992. A multi-use pavilion was soon added, enabling Tennis Club members to enjoy all year round playing and changing facilities.

The Club is affiliated to the Lawn Tennis Association and caters for juniors, students as well as family members. Coaching is available for adults and juniors, either individually or in groups.

Tapestry Group

Dorothy Leavey, Carol Taylor and Edna Fletcher

The Tapestry Group, formed in 1990, spent 1999 completing work on a millennium project to provide 11 prayer kneelers for the parish church, seven across the communion rail and four for use in the sanctuary. A series of tea parties organised by Ruth Roberts in 1997 raised £240, enabling the ten lady members of the group to begin work on the kneelers, working to a pattern designed by Dorothy Leavey copied from tiles in the church sanctuary.

The group members: Dorothy Leavey, Pauline Bedhall, Christine Fletcher, Beryl Withington, Edna Fletcher, Kathleen Knight, Mollie Loach, Carol Taylor, Diane Taylor and Ruth Roberts, met together on Wednesday mornings to complete their task.

Clifton Wanderers

The Clifton Wanderers was formed in 1999 as an informal walking group whose aim is to enjoy and maintain local footpaths, continuing the work of the Clifton Rambling Group that was started in 1977 by a group of Saxon Close residents.

The year also saw the publication of Walks Around Clifton-upon-Teme, one of a series of walking guides produced jointly by the Parish Council and Worcestershire County Council. The guide features seven walks beginning and ending in the village, each with a map and directions, and was compiled with the assistance of several residents, including Derek Leavey, local Footpaths Officer since 1995, and Lyn Emery, organiser of the Clifton Wanderers.

Rainbows

The eight members of the Clifton Rainbow Guides, led by their Guider-in-charge Jackie Holloway, continued their regular weekly meetings in the BP Hut. The Rainbow Guides start from five years old, moving to the Brownies when the reach the age of seven.

Brownies

The 1st Clifton-on-Teme Brownies numbered 13 members during 1999. One of their biggest achievements was helping the Guides renovate the BP Hut, including the kitchen and toilets. Under the leadership of Brown Owl, Eileen Richmond, and Unit Helper Jenny Pound, the group's activities included attendance at the annual Remembrance Sunday parade in November.

Guides

The 1st Clifton-on-Teme Guides have been in existence for the past 27 years and the eight members were again involved in a variety of community projects, including helping to keep the church clean, organising a 'get a grip on litter' campaign around the village and making Christmas gifts for the Friendship Club as well as taking part in the Remembrance Sunday parade with the Brownies. Led by Helen Winder and Eileen Richmond, the Guides - aged between 10 and 14 years - meet regularly in the BP Hut by the Recreation Ground.

Pony Club

The Clifton-on-Teme Hunt branch of the Pony Club has been teaching local children to ride for the past 46 years. Affiliated to the British Horse Society, the Pony Club organises rallies, hunter trialsone-day events and the annual summer camp, again held on the Malvern showground with their District Commissioner Bunty Crump. The 35 members cook their meals around a camp fire and sleep in one block of stables while their ponies sleep in another.

Clifton-on-Teme Hunt

The Clifton Hunt is one of the youngest in England, founded by local farmers in 1926. The hunt kennels were originally at Shelsley Walsh near the Kennel Bend on the Hill Climb track. The opening meet is always held on the village green in Clifton in November, and on New Year's Day the hounds meet again at the New Inn. The Hunt also organises the Clifton Point-to-Point races at Upper Sapey in the spring.

Clifton Playing Field Association

As recently as the late 1980s there were few sports and play facilities in the village. In December 1988 the inaugural meeting of the Clifton Playing Field Association (CPFA) was held in order to progress development of the Recreation Field owned by the Parish Council and located in Pound Lane. A committee was formed and several years of intense fund-raising followed in an effort to raise money for the project.

By 1992, a further area of land adjoining the field was purchased in order to incorporate a football pitch. Early work was begun by Bert Bradley; the tennis courts were completed by September and the football pitch levelled in October. A tree planting scheme the following year saw more than 250 trees planted in the area. In April 1993, a further grant of £60,000 from the Foundation for Sport and the Arts enabled the pavilion to be completed, officially opened in 1994.

The football pitch was ready for the first match in September 1995, while Bernard Pound and Neil Sparey completed work on the children's play area and the bowling green made ready for use in 1996. When, finally, work on the car parking area was finished, the entire project had been brought to fruition.

The CPFA is still repaying a £15,000 loan from the Parish Council, much of which is raised by local residents.

Bowling Club

The Clifton-upon-Teme Bowling Club was formed in 1994 when the green was created on the Recreation Ground. It was two years later that the members were able to play on their own green, however, and by 1999 the club's 30 members competed in some 26 friendly matches with other clubs throughout the West Midlands. The Club Chairman, Eddie Thompson, was one of the founding members and has looked after the green since it was laid. His wife Marie is Club Captain.

Clifton Rovers

Clifton Rovers Football Club gained promotion to Worcester's Sunday premier league in 1999 for the first time in the club's long history going back more than 100 years. The Club decided not to field a team for the 1999/2000 season, however.

Handbell Ringers

The Clifton Handbell Ringers formed 22 years ago at the suggestion of the Rev. Donald Heggie, then vicar of Clifton and the Shelsley parishes, who had come across some handbells at Shelsley that were not being used. Over a period of several years, funds were raised for the purchase of the set of 22 bells now used by the group of seven women who regularly give performances at local nursing homes and sheltered accommodation in the area as well as other venues. The leader is Pat Bradley, while Chris House and Jackie Gilbert are the only two remaining members of the original group from 1978.

Women's Institute

The Clifton branch of the Women's Institute was formed as recently as 1965. One of its founding members and first President, Elizabeth Daniel, says "we were surprised to find that there had never been a WI in the village." Elizabeth is still a member of the branch, which continues to offer a varied programme of lectures and talks on a wide range of topics as well as organising occasional outings. The current WI President, Patricia Collett, was particularly pleased that the branch was asked to provide the catering for both a diamond wedding and a golden wedding in 1999.

Friendship Club

The Friendship Club was formed in 1971 to provide an opportunity for local residents over the age of 60 to meet, exchange ideas and socialise on a regular basis. Its first leader was Barbara Thompson; 28 years later, the club still has one founder member, 91-year-old Edna Fletcher, attending regularly.

In 1999, the Friendship Club was jointly led by Marie Thompson and Ann MacBryde, meeting on the first and third Wednesday of each month in the Village Hall. In the summer months, members often meet in one another's homes as well as going on outings together. A club tradition is the mini-market on the village green on the first Saturday in September.

"We are a friendly, relaxed and happy group and welcome anyone, male or female, approaching 60 to join us," says Ann MacBryde. "We are flexible with our lower age limit these days and as far as an upper age limit, well, our oldest, and very active member is 'Cissie' Devereaux aged 95!"

Friendship Club on the village green, September 1999

Clifton Gardeners

Clifton Gardeners was formed by a group of villagers in 1996 when the village ceased to enter the annual Britain in Bloom competition following a remarkable five year series of success.

Chaired by Colin White, the group aims to continue the village's carefully maintained appearance, looking after the flower beds and tubs put in place by the team involved in Clifton's successful entries in the Britain in Bloom competition. It also raises money for village groups and other charities as a result of the annual Open Gardens day. The group aims to organise informative and interesting activities both for its members and a wider village audience.

Clifton-upon-Teme and Lower Sapey Conservative Branch

The local Conservative branch was formed in 1949 at a meeting in the Lion Inn. Mrs Molly Skyrme became secretary soon afterwards, a position she has held for over 50 years. The branch still meets regularly at the Lion, chaired by Anne Speed.

Clifton-upon-Teme and Sapey Common
January 1st 2000

The Village (East side)

The Lion Inn was originally the Guildhall or meeting house in the village; also referred to as the manor house and used as a court house. The original building, parts of which still survive, dates back to the 13th century and consisted of a great hall with a central fireplace. Around the courtyard at the back of the building were the granaries, sheds for cattle and other outbuildings. It is likely that it was always used as a hostelry for travellers, later

becoming an inn before 1600 when it was known as the Red Lion after the coat of arms of the Jeffreyes family of Homme Castle.

The Lion Inn team

The Lion Inn has been run by Richard and Jayne Redfern for three years, during which time they have acquired a reputation for serving good home-cooked food and real ales. Richard also supplies beer via the internet. They organised special millennium celebrations on New Year's Eve, including a spectacular fireworks display on the village green at midnight. Their daughters, Claire and Philippa, attend the local school's.

Lion Courtyard

Former owners of the Lion Inn, Richard and Anne Speed, now live at **The Old Stable** behind the inn, having come to Clifton in 1980. Dick was Clerk to the Parish Council and Secretary of the PCC for many years; he has been Captain of the Clifton bell ringers for several years as well as treasurer of the local Conservative branch and a member of the village hall management team. Anne is actively involved with many facets of village life; in addition to the bell-ringers, PCC and village hall committee, she was a member of the St. Kenelm's choir that performed Fauré's Requiem in 1999.

When retired teacher Phyllis Barnett moved into **High View** ten years ago, she was one of the first occupants of the converted buildings in the Lion courtyard.

Alan and Alana Cooper at **2 Stable Cottage** are a brother and sister entertainment act who've lived in Clifton for three years, but spend most of their time working on cruise ships owned by Princess Cruises, the American division of P&O, where they have been for the past 12 years.

Mark Baker and Jane James moved into **Stock Cottage** in 1999.

The Granary was let to Tina Evans, daughter of Herbert Yeomans, at the end of 1999.

Lion Cottage, adjoining the Lion Inn has been occupied by Janet Lawrence since she gave up running the Lion ten years ago. She particularly remembers breaking her ankle in September 1999 and having to get around on crutches, including collecting the money for the Clifton Playing Fields Association monthly draw. [The name Lion Cottage originally belonged to 'Goodwood' on the corner of Pound Lane]

High school teacher Tim Dyson and accountant Zoë Thomas have lived next door at **Kindly** since 1996 in what was once the village Post Office. In its time, the building has also been used as the police station and Foyles lending library where, during the war, local residents could borrow books from the shelves that lined the front porch for one penny.

David Graham and Rosemary Collie

David Graham and Rosemary Collie moved to **Yew Tree Cottage** just over two years ago, having spent the last few years working for charities in Africa and Central America. They still like to travel and 1999 was marked by a memorable trip to India. Closer to home, David and Rosemary like walking and cycling and particularly enjoy the countryside surrounding Clifton, "though some of the hills are a bit of a challenge on a bike," says Rosemary. They both work locally although Rosemary used to commute to Birmingham. David's leadwork adorns a number of buildings in Worcester. Rosemary is Operations Manager for an educational travel company in Malvern. She has also been a member of the team who produced this book. The house is often referred to as the 'Webb's' house, after the Webb family who moved there in 1947, remaining until the 1980s since when it has changed hands several times until Rosemary and David arrived in 1997. The Webb family lived in the village for many years, at one time owning the shop that once occupied part of The Old Smithy opposite.

The garden at **Hope Wynd** is a good indication of just how enthusiastic Colin and Elizabeth White are about their gardening. Elizabeth's hobby is propagating unusual perennial plants, many of which she sells to raise money for her favourite good causes, while Colin is the chairman of the Clifton Gardeners, the group formed to maintain the standards set by the village's five successful bids for the regional Britain in Bloom award. The couple run two businesses from their home, a former estate cottage dating from the 18th century. Colin, a business consultant, and Elizabeth manage 'Countryways', their holiday cottage business based on Hopeway Cottage located in the garden at Hope Wynd.

Elizabeth Whit

Number **11**, home of Doris Lumby for many years, lay empty at the end of 1999, having been bought by Robert Butterworth.

Stan and Jean Dennis at number **15** say they are lucky to have their son Mark and his young family living nearby in Saxon Close. Jean, born at Pitlands Farm, is still remembered for the fruit and vegetables she sold from the backdoor of her house for many years until 1990. Now her eldest grand-daughter is a pupil at the village school that she herself attended 60 years ago, and Jean helps with the Mother and Toddler group that her younger grand-daughter joins when she is not at nursery school. Jean and her husband Stan, a retired engineer, were dismayed when Clifton Rovers football club closed earlier in the year because of difficulty finding enough players to make the team. "We really miss watching the local team play on Sunday mornings, having been Clifton Rovers supporters all our lives," said Stan.

Tudor Cottage has been home to Bernard and Vera Rowley for 20 years.

Next door, at **Flint Cottage** lives Lesley Rogers.

Nick and Tracie Haywood bought **Oak House** adjoining the Post Office in 1999 where they live with their daughter Lucinda, age four, and son George, age three. Nick and his two brothers took over the family building firm of Haywood & Sons from father Phil in 1999. Tracie, who moved to Clifton 14 years ago when her mother, Janet Lawrence, took over the Lion, works part-time in the Post Office where her mother-in-law June Haywood is now the sub-postmistress. Tracie enjoys being a member of the extended Haywood family: "The children benefit from having so many relatives living nearby," she says. "They also have the advantage of a small village school that both their father Nick and grandfather Phil Haywood attended as well."

Post Office

The first mention of a Post Office in Clifton was in June 1898 when a letter was sent to the Postmaster general asking if a telegraph office could be set up in the village. But as early as 1870, mail for the village was brought up from Whitbourne by postman Matthew Bund whose route covered 16 miles on foot across fields and through woods. In due course, Fred Hall at the General Stores became the first sub-postmaster, assisted by his sister-in-law, Miss Kate Bishop, who sold stamps from a small office on the right of the shop. When Fred Hall and his son were tragically killed in an air crash in 1934 the shop was sold and Miss Bishop became the sub-postmistress, moving to 'Kindly' (now number 5 The Village), a post she held for over 30 years with the help of Bunty Ennion's mother. When Miss Bishop retired, Alice Trow at the Oak House became the village sub-postmistress for ten years until Bob Pearce took over the role. He retired in 1986 and June Haywood, the present sub-postmistress, bought Oak House. The date 1721 can be seen carved in the beam over the present Post Office doorway.

The Post Office team (from left): Doreen MacLean, Mike Earthey, June Haywood, Andrew Thompson, Ken Tolly, Roy Done and Tracie Haywood

Oak Cottage has been home to cellist Corinne Snoad and her children, Christian (14) and Joshua (11) for six years. As well as performing at home and abroad with the CBSO, Corinne has a number of pupils to whom she gives cello lessons. In addition, she runs the monthly ladies' bible study group in the village and has also recently started a weekly school prayer group.

Cleaver Cottage is occupied by company director Nigel Duffield.

Behind, at **Bakery Cottage**, live Frank and Sheila Burgoyne, retired farmers who arrived in Clifton nearly two years ago. Sheila enjoys art classes with the Friendship Club.

Peter and Beverley Richards and children outside the General Stores

The new owners of the **General Stores**, Peter and Beverley Richards, say they have been made very welcome since arriving in August 1999. They both gave up careers to take over the business after moving from Welland. Their children, Laura and Tom, both attend the village school.

John and Elizabeth Cowmeadow live at number **29**.

At **Unicorn Cottage**, once part of the Unicorn Inn in Clifton, David and Maureen Rouse celebrated their ruby wedding anniversary in 1999. The couple have lived in the village for 21 years, originally running the General Stores until moving to their present address 17 years ago and David now works locally as a gardener.

Old Unicorn Cottage, the other half of what was the Unicorn Inn until the late 1800s, is the home of Mike and Angie Pagett. The building dates back to the 17th century when the inn was known as the Bunch of Grapes, changing its name to the Unicorn sometime between 1821 and 1839 - influenced, perhaps, by the popular children's nursery rhyme of the time as the other two inns in the village were the Lion and the Crown. There are still a few features of the original inn inside. "I've had a fascinating time discovering the old behind the modern additions and restoring it as much as possible to its original state," says Angie who issues the 'Grapevine', an information sheet for newcomers to the village giving details of local activities and facilities. The 'Grapevine' was started by three Clifton residents in 1991

Mike and Angie Pagett

Next door, at number **35**, lives Lorraine Harris with her 15-year-old daughter Stephanie and 13-year-old son Christopher. Lorraine is company secretary to Midland Tree Care, run by Jenny Haywood in Hope Lane. Both her children are members of Clifton Pony Club and Martley Young Farmers.

Elizabeth Daniel

Elizabeth Daniel and her daughter Caroline have been at **Chapel House** since returning to Clifton in 1980 after an absence of ten years, having previously owned the Old House (now occupied by George and Jean Young) from 1963 until 1970. Elizabeth, whose husband Leslie died in 1993, has been an exceptionally active member of church and WI activities in the village for many years, but stresses the enormous amount of work done for St. Kenelm's every week of the year by local people who undertake such duties as sidesmen, readers, flower arrangers, cleaning, maintaining the fabric and churchyard and helping with refreshments. Chapel House dates back to the 18th century when it was originally used as a Wesleyan Chapel.

Albert and Flo Jones have lived in Clifton for most of their lives, the last 18 years at number **39**, one of the very few remaining farm workers' cottages in the parish, belonging to Salford Court Farm where Albert is employed.

Andrew and Wendy Bradley at **Broadfields** both celebrated their 40th birthday in 1999, having lived in their present home for 11 years. Andrew, a plant hire contractor, has lived in the village all his life and moved house five times. Wendy is a personnel officer and the couple have two sons, Thomas and William.

Phil Nuthall outside the Old Police House

The **Old Police House** was built in 1934 and has been occupied by Philip and Heather Nuthall since 1971. Phil, a former uniformed officer, now has a civilian post within the West Mercia Police information development department at Worcester. Since arriving in the village, Phil helped start a Cub Scout pack in 1972 which eventually led to the creation of a Scout troop. He was appointed Assistant County Commissioner for the Scout movement in the early 1990s.

The first recorded Police Constable in Clifton was James Dovey, appointed in 1845. The 1861 census records that Pc Samuel Michael was stationed there, followed by Eli Edwards who appears in the 1881 census returns for the village aged 38. He was followed by Pc Edwin Spragg who remained until 1904, the father of ten children. In 1896, Robert Hill is also shown as the sergeant-in-charge of the Police Station in the village. The next recorded police officer in the parish is George Henry Powis Benbow between 1930 and 1933, followed by Pc Edwin Reginald Dentist, the first incumbent of the new Police House in 1934, and Pc Arthur Mann in 1939 who remained in Clifton until 1952. He was followed by at least five police officers, including Bill Norman, Eddy Hobday, Joe Barns, Dave Barker, Dave Gardiner and Charlie Rowley. Phil Nuthall took over in August 1971, serving as the last police constable in the village when the beat was abolished in 1989 when he moved to Kidderminster and later West Mercia Police Headquarters near Worcester until he retired in November 1998.

Teme House (formerly 'Pelicans') is the home of Alan and Maria Flower and their children Oliver, Amelia and William. Alan, a software architect, campaigned unsuccessfully against the proposed housing development in Hope Lane in 1999.

Clive and Helen Studd have lived at **The Manor House** for nine years. Both are Consultant Anaesthetists working at Worcester Royal Infirmary where Clive is Chairman of the Anaesthetic department. Helen specialises in anaesthesia for vascular surgery. The house, which is Grade II listed, lies within the village conservation area and dates from 17th century. Since then there have been a number of major extensions including the addition of a Georgian main facade.

Brian and Pat Crooks moved to **Steps Farm** with daughters Paula and Nicola from the Flint House in 1983, after buying the 17th century farmhouse from the Winnington estate. The farm itself is owned by the Brockhill Estate and is farmed by Ian Sparey who lives at Otheridge Pool Cottage.

The Byre, behind Steps Farm, has been occupied by retired couple, Ronald and Sylvia Bradburn, since they converted the building themselves three years ago.

The Bungalow at Steps Farm is the home of agricultural engineer Robert How, Jane Bradley and Jane's seven-year-old son Sam. Jane's parents live at Broadlands in the Old Road.

Neil and Anne Sparey and their three children, Luke, Charlotte and Tabatha have lived at **Oak Barn** behind Steps Farm for ten years. Neil, a design engineer, runs his agricultural and industrial engineering business, NDS Engineering, from home, designing and making special purpose machinery, much of it in use locally. Both Neil and Anne are members of the Tennis Club and the CPFA. They particularly remember watching the eclipse in August and their dalmation bitch giving birth to a litter of eight puppies in 1999. Anne's mother Jean Benning lives in Saxon Close.

Zbigniew, Milada and David Tarka moved into **The Old Granary** at Steps Farm in 1999, having arrived from Australia. Polish born Zbigmiew and Milada from Czechoslovakia lived in Australia for 19 years before coming to Clifton. Zbigmiew is general manager of a petroleum and chemical industry equipment manufacturer while Milada teaches music at King's School and the sixth form college in Worcester as well as helping with reading at Clifton school. Both think the village has "lots of character" and enjoy the glorious sunsets. Their son now works at the village shop.

The Village (West side)

Goodwood (formerly Lion Cottage) is owned by Phil and June Haywood but was unoccupied at the end of 1999.

Brian Hoare and Michael Brookes

Since retiring and moving to **Greenholme** overlooking the village green nearly four years ago, Brian Hoare and Michael Brookes have become involved with the local British Legion branch, the Friendship Club, the Clifton Gardeners and the PCC. Brian is also a member of the Village Hall committee and Michael a member of the St. Kenelm's choir. In addition, they were both involved with the Flower Festival, the Motorcycle Show and the Poetry and Music evening during 1999.

Next door, at number **6 The Green** (once known as Laburnam Cottage), retired Defence official Max Hemming enjoyed a particularly successful year's golf at Sapey golf club in 1999 where he is the Seniors' golf captain, winning the Club's mixed open tournament in May with his partner Paula Gordon. Max's parents first bought the house 26 years ago, and he settled back there in 1986 after returning from the Sultinate of Oman where he was employed by the Oman Ministry of Defence with the rank of Major.

Clifton Primary School

The first school in Clifton was started in 1844. At the time, many parents were reluctant to send their children to the school, preferring instead to keep them at home where they could be of help. A weekly payment of one penny was required. By 1855, the National School as it was known, run by Frederick Noad and his wife Lucy, a sewing mistress, had 75 pupils and was supported by voluntary contributions.

Bury's Place at the top of Hope Lane has been the home of John Fletcher since 1976, although he moved to Clifton with his family 31 years ago. His many business interests include Clifton Engineering, the gas heater manufacturing company based at the 'Green Garage' at the top of the Old Road and run by his son Mark. Now chairman of Ambi-Rad, the company he formed in 1979, John is also a keen collector and restorer of 'curious' cars, having amassed a remarkable collection that includes the 1923 Scott Sociable three-wheeler (one of only five surviving). In 1999, he acquired several military vehicles, a 1912 Model T Ford in original condition, and a rare 1939 SS100 Jaguar 2-seater sports car.

John Fletcher in his 1939 SS100 Jaguar outside Bury's Place

Bury's Place, which John shares with his partner Rachel and her daughters Stephanie and Pennie, was extensively renovated and restored in the late 1970s. The building, which dates back to the 17th century, was the village butcher's shop for many years.

Charles and Patricia Knowles

The Old Smithy, overlooking the chestnut tree in the centre of the village, is the home of retired consultant orthodontist Charles Knowles and his wife Patricia. Since moving to Clifton from Devon eight years ago, both have been actively involved in village activities in 1999, including the Flower Festival and the Church.

The 17th century **Crown House** next door has been occupied by Jerry and Sue Johns since 1975. Before they moved in, it had been variously a fish and chip shop, general stores run by the Lewis family, and - until around 1860 - the Crown Inn. While Sue carried on with her job at St. Richard's preparatory school in Bredenbury in 1999, Jerry left the BBC to begin a new publishing venture, the Crown House Press from his office overlooking the garden of their home. Both their sons are former pupils of the village school and have since moved away. Jamie married his Romanian wife Elena at The Birche in Shelsley Beauchamp in May, and his younger brother Barnaby returned from Japan for the occasion.

Sue and Jerry Johns

George and Jean Young

The other end of the Crown House is **Crown Cottage**, the home of Charlotte Moyle and her daughters India and Iona who both became pupils at St. Richard's in September.

At the **Old House**, believed to be the oldest house in the village, retired Brigadier George Young MBE and his wife Jean spent their 30th year in the village. Now in their 80s, both have been active members of the local branch of the British Legion of which George is the President.

Next door at number **22** live Roger Gaydon, an engineering buyer, and his wife Anne, a school secretary, with sons Robert and James, who are involved with both the Tennis Club and the CPFA.

Eddie and Marie Thompson, daughter Jane and baby Holly

Eddie and Marie Thompson have occupied the neighbouring pair of 17th century cottages that are numbered **24** and **26** since moving from Tenbury in 1966. They now live in the part numbered 26, while daughter Jane shares the other half with husband Mark Dayson and baby daughter Holly. Both Eddie and Marie have been enthusiastic members of many village activities and organisations, including the Bowling Club, the British Legion and the Clifton Playing Field Association (Eddie was the CPFA's first Chairman), but they are probably best known as the driving force behind the Clifton in Bloom campaign which saw the village win the Best Village category six years running between 1990 and 1995. More recently, the couple have devoted their energy to the Bowling Club which they helped found five years ago; Marie as Club Captain and Eddie as Chairman, winning the Men's Open and Mixed Singles tournament in 1999. Now in his 60s, Eddie still puts in a full day's work helping John Fletcher at Bury's Place and still finding time to restore a Riley Elf once owned by Rose Bethall's father, Dick Roberts. Their son Andrew, now living with his wife and two young sons in Martley, has the distinction of being the village's youngest ever postman.

Retired post-woman 'Bunty' Ennion and her sister Joan Warren at number **28**, opposite the Post Office, originally came to Clifton with their parents in 1939. Joan left the village after she got married in 1968, returning in 1989 to live with her sister. The local postmen still call on them every morning for a cup of tea at the end of their rounds.

'Bunty' Ennion

The Wakefield family at **Clematis Cottage** are all active members of village life. Paul, a business development manager for a Worcestershire print and design company, is a former Chairman and founder-member of the Clifton Tennis Club; Sally is a classroom assistant at Clifton School, having formed the first pre-school play group there, and their three children James, Emily and Alice have all attended the school.

The **Veterinary Surgery** adjoining Clematis Cottage was set up in the village in 1996 by the Ludlow-based Teme Veterinary Practice. The surgery, which is open part-time every day, is manned by one vet, usually Rodney Brereton, and receptionist/nurse Gill Whiteman.

Ian and Jane Watson came to **Hope Cottage** with their daughter Annie three years ago, welcoming the addition of baby Daniel in June 1999. Jane, a speech and language therapist enjoys attending the Mums and Toddler group in the village. Ian is a project manager.

Newcomers Neil and Hilary Higton moved to **Hoppe Croft** with their three daughters from Birmingham in 1998. While Neil runs a successful computer business in South Birmingham, Hilary combines her job as a midwife in Redditch with looking after her children and leading the Toddler Group in the village. In 1999 she also became a Governor of Clifton-on-Teme Primary School. Both Neil and Hilary are members of Clifton Tennis Club, and their daughters Esther, Naomi and Lydia attend the Rainbows and Brownies group. "We were attracted to Clifton for many reasons," says Hilary. "The school and the warm, friendly community made us realise it would be a place we could happily settle as a family."

Chartered surveyors Steven and Sarah Tromans moved into **Highgate House** nearly three years ago with young sons, Jack and William, attracted by the fact that Clifton had a school, a shop and a pub. Both are members of the CPFA.

Next door, number **42** has been the home of Bunny and Janet Hooper for the past 45 years. Bunny (real name Ronald, but known to all as Bunny since childhood) has worked for the Winnington estate for 54 years. Janet was born in the Crown House.

The Nook was originally three cottages until they were later converted to one dwelling and is now occupied by Jill Yeomans whose late husband Herbert, former owner of the garage, came to live there 24 years ago.

Mrs Violet Lewis at number **46** is the oldest member of the Lewis family who kept Lewis's Stores for many years at what is now the Crown House. Her son, Bernard, and daughter, Sue Palmer, still live in the village. She moved into her present home in 1983 which then belonged to Herbert Yeomans who had the prefabricated wooden bungalow built there in 1947.

Mark and Tyrone Phillips with father Tony (centre)

Yeomans Garage was sold to Tyrone and Mark Phillips by Herbert Yeomans in 1986 and continues to provide a vehicle sales service, MoTs, repairs and a 24 hour recovery service.

Herbert Yeomans came to live at Homme Castle in 1927 with his father and brother Jack who later farmed at Salford Court. After serving in the Royal Navy during the war, Herbert bought Martin's Cottage, a derelict building on land opposite the police station in Clifton which he gradually developed as the garage business that still continues. Herbert died in 1996 at the age of 80.

Church Road

The annual sale of Christmas trees at **Walnut Lodge**, between the Church and the Lion Inn courtyard, attracted plenty of custom as usual at the end of 1999. Tim Roscoe has been planting and selling Christmas trees ever since he and Sue moved there in 1978 and reckons he has probably grown around 18,000 on his land behind the house. In addition to his job as a sales manager for a fire protection company, he recently developed a small trade in fir-cones. Sue, a French teacher at a Worcester preparatory school is also a member of the Clifton Handbell Ringers. Of their three children, Simon still lives with them while Toby is in Australia and Sarah in Cambridge.

Tim Roscoe and assistant outside Walnut Lodge, Christmas 1999

St. Kenelm's Church

The Reverend Clifford Owen moved into **The Rectory** with his family in July 1989 on his appointment as rector of the three parishes of Clifton, Lower Sapey and the Shelsleys. Author of Baptise Every Baby? and editor of Reforming Infant Baptism, Clifford is an active supporter of the Movement for the Reform of Infant Baptism. As Diocesan Ecumenical Officer, about one third of his time is devoted to ecumenical duties within the diocese in addition to his pastoral work within the three parishes. His wife Avis who retired from teaching three years ago, is now an archives assistant at the Worcestershire County Record Office. Their two daughters, Kathryn (16) and Isobel (14) live with them, while their sons John and Charles are both in London, the latter a concert pianist frequently giving recitals in the area.

The old vicarage, now Burleigh Court

Burleigh Court, the former parish vicarage, has been the home of John and Lyn Leask since 1977 when it was replaced by the present rectory. Built in 1840, it retains the original stable block and a cottage dating back to the 1540s that accommodated the vicarage staff in earlier years and, more recently was used as the village surgery. An unusual weeping lime tree in the large garden flowers in July is particularly attractive to bees and John, a keen bee keeper, often produces lime honey from the flowers. "It's not unusual for young couples wishing to get married to knock on the door, hoping to get some advice on what they should do," he says. "While I'm happy to give them the benefit of my advice, I always direct them next door."

Forge House, opposite the Lion Inn, has been converted into two dwellings, one occupied by Howard and Margaret Thomas, and the other, **Forge Flat** by tree contractor Steve Butler and Jackie Tingle, a scientific officer. Steve used to play for Clifton Rovers and was hoping to start a new football team in the village in 2000. Steve's father Alan lives in Kenelm Close.

A blacksmith's shop for many years, **The Old Forge** was converted in 1993 into what is now the home of Phil and June Haywood who moved across the yard from Forge House where their family had lived for most of the last century. The building still retains many features of the original smithy, including the iron bars at the windows and the stable door which has a copy of the Church door handle, said to be the largest in the county. The date on the front of the building is 1874. Since taking over the business from his father in 1970, Phil has built more than 30 houses in and around the village, including Forge Meadows, as well as many agricultural buildings. All four sons live in the area; Tom, Nick and Matthew who have taken over the family firm of Haywood & Sons, and Jeremy. June Haywood has been the sub-postmistress in Clifton for many years and conceived the idea of producing a book about the village to mark the Millennium, a project she has led throughout 1999.

(L-R) Tom, Nick, father Phil and Matthew Haywood

The Haywood family is the oldest in Clifton, dating back to the 17th century when it occupied Salford Court for several years. The tombs of many Haywood ancestors can be seen outside St. Kenelms church. Phil Haywood's great grandfather, Ernest Haywood, left Forge House and the family business to his son Ernest on his death in 1926. When he eventually died in 1951, his wife Edith took over, running the business with the help of brother George, a blacksmith and agricultural engineer. George Haywood married Nellie Good, a teacher at Clifton school, in 1926 and the couple had two sons, Philip and Leslie. In due course, Philip and his father George raised the money to buy the business themselves, thus keeping Forge House, the adjoining cottage (Goodwood) and the yard and field together. Father and son continued the building and agricultural engineering business together until George Haywood's death in 1970, since when Philip has continued, assisted in recent years by his sons, three of whom took over the family business when he finally retired in 1999. Today there are 15 people with the Haywood surname living in Clifton, all of whom are related. Bertha Haywood at Keeper's Cottage, for example, is the widow of Frank Haywood.

At **The Anchorage**, next to the Old Forge, live Kate Harper, Michael Earthey and Kate's son Stuart. Kate has lived in Clifton since moving to Little Paddock in the Old Road 31 years ago and was a Parish Councillor for several years until she resigned in 1999 but, despite suffering from health problems, continued to take an active part in village activities. Both she and Mick, the Clifton and Upper Sapey postman, organised several quiz nights at the Lion Inn in aid of the Clifton playing field and Mick is also a member of the team producing this book.

Birchfield House is home to the Cripps family, Roger and Sue and students Luisa and Richard. Sue has fond memories of her children's schooldays in Clifton: "the hilarious Christmas plays and the Christmas lunches cooked by a band of mums, partly at home and partly at school, and served to children and staff. I feel that all the children there had a wonderful fun-packed village school background which can only be of benefit to them now."

Lilian Williams came to Clifton 25 years ago when she and her late husband Bill retired from teaching, moving into **Desford** opposite the church after Phil Haywood's mother had moved to Goodwood, the cottage on the corner of Pound Lane. The bungalow was actually built by Phil for he and June to live in when they married in 1958.

Church Road c1930

Next door, at **Keeper's Cottage** lives one of Clifton's older residents, 89-year-old Bertha Haywood. Now the oldest member of the Haywood family, Bertha's friends and family are close at hand. Her home is filled with photographs and memories of her brothers and her late husband Frank, for many years gamekeeper to Sir Francis Winnington. Born at Stanford Bridge, she and Frank married in 1935 and moved to Keepers Cottage in 1937 where she has lived ever since.

At **2 Church Row**, 69-year-old Mrs Jo Powell lives with daughter Beverley and her partner, Paul Franklin. Jo spent her childhood at Pitlands, a time, she recalls, of tending paraffin lamps and carrying milk up to the village. She moved to her present home more than forty years ago when she married her late husband John. Each New Year's Eve, she opens a window "to let the old year out" and opens the front door "to let the new year in, just like my parents did at Pitlands all those years ago."

Michael Brooksbank who moved into **2 Church Cottages** in July 1999 is an Operations Manager for a design and manufacture consultancy specialising in aero-structures and nuclear engineering.

When Ted and Peggy Hooper moved to **Church Cottage** in 1961 from Manor Road, Peggy's parents, Stan and Mary Jones, moved in next door. Peggy's family originally lived in one of the three cottages that formed The Nook now occupied by Jill Yeomans. Two years after her birth there, Peggy, one of six children, and her family moved to Old Unicorn Cottage, then owned by George Burnham of Burnham's Buses. She married Ted in 1968. Peggy's son Neil now lives in Worcester, and their daughter Angela at Shelsley. Peggy was the village school caretaker for over 25 years until 1997, achieving the remarkable record of never having a single day off sick.

Churchlands has been the home of Mary Parsons since she had it built 36 years ago, nearly ten years after first moving the Clifton. Now retired, Mary was Head of English at the former Girls' Grammar School in Worcester for 20 years, and later became chairman of the Clifton Primary School. Since retiring from full-time teaching, she has had several studies of literary text published in addition to writing the history of the Worcester Choral Society. Mary recalls that when she first moved to the village in the early 1950s, some local residents still had no mains water supply and drew their water in buckets from one of several stand-pipes, one of which remains on the green. "Farming was less mechanised, and there were many more agricultural workers living in the village," she says. "There were many hop fields in the area, and a number of villagers were occupied picking and drying hops by traditional hand method in September each year." .

One of Diana Taylor's less pleasant memories of 1999 was when **Kenelm Cottage**, her home for the past ten years was flooded following an exceptionally heavy downpour of rain in April. The house was originally two cottages and was formerly known as Rose Villa.

Christine Brookes came to live at **Enderley** with her father from Edgbaston more than 20 years ago. A keen horsewoman, she is an enthusiastic follower of the Clifton-on-Teme Hunt.

Keith and Rose Hollings have lived at **Clifton Lodge**, the first house on the left at the approach to the village, since 1984. Clifton Lodge was originally occupied by the manager of the Winnington estate.

Martyn and Bunty Crump moved to **Church House Farm** 30 years ago when Martyn took over the tenancy from Bunty's father, Don Parker, the fourth generation of his family to farm there. The precise age of the building is uncertain, but a receipt for parish rates dated 1779 was recently discovered in a beam inside the farmhouse. Martyn now farms the 210 acres with his son Robert who also lives at Church House with his wife Brenda, a florist, and sons Tom and Joe. In 1999 they managed cattle, sheep and arable crops of wheat, barley and oats. For the Crump family, 1999 was memorable for the arrival of their third grandchild Rosemarie the previous Christmas, daughter of Martyn and Bunty's daughter Brigette. In addition, Robert passed his HGV driving test and bought a lorry enabling him to diversify by becoming a hay and straw merchant. Bunty has lived in Clifton all her life, in the course of which she has served as a Parish Councillor, helped start the guides group in the village and for many years organised Clifton Pony Club events at Church House Farm. She is now a governor of Clifton school and a member of the team producing this book.

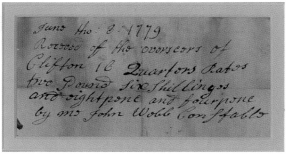

1779 receipt found inside Church House Farm

Martyn and Bunty Crump with their family

Manor Road

The first 12 houses in Manor Road were built in 1946. Others were added in the late 1960s.

Bernie Lewis

1 Manor Road is occupied by Bernard and Pat Lewis and daughter Jodie. Bernard's collection of old photographs of Clifton has made him an invaluable member of the team producing this book, though he was also involved with the Classic Motorcycle Show in August. Pat is a qualified reflexologist, masseur and healer.

Simon and Karen Bullock returned to the village in 1999 after eight years away, moving into **2 Manor Road** in November with their children Carly, Paul and Roxanne, followed shortly afterwards by the arrival of baby Peter on 29th December. Simon's mother Margaret sadly died in July. "Since we have come back, everyone has made us so welcome," says Simon.

When Lawson and Pauline Bullock first came to live in Clifton 39 years ago, they rented the Knoll bungalow above Hill Farm where Lawson worked for 17 years, moving to **3 Manor Road** in 1975 where they now live happily in retirement. Of their five children, son Frank lives with them while daughter Cathine and her husband Dave Merry are a few doors away at number 12. Lawson's brother Bill lives in the Old Road.

Dave and Rose Bethell have lived at **4 Manor Road** for more than 20 years. Rose was born at number 6 Manor Road. Her father Dick Roberts, who died in May 1999 at the age of 81, was a local church verger and bell-ringer as well as making coffins for Ernest Haywood the village undertaker. Their son Steven, working for a marine rope-making firm in Malvern, returned recently to live in Clifton after an absence of six years.

Molly Wilson (left) and 'Dolly' Coldicott

At **5 Manor Road** with her partner John Coldicott, Jackie Holloway looked back on 1999 with pride as Secretary and Ladies' Captain of the Clifton Tennis Club, having collected the ladies' tennis team trophy at a LTA dinner after coming top of their division. She has two daughters, Jennifer (14) and Lauren (11). John's grandmother lives at number 6.

'Dolly' Coldicott at **6 Manor Road** was born at one of the Ham Farm cottages in 1921, just six months after her schoolfriend Molly Wilson who she later came to live near in Manor Road in the 1950s after marrying her husband Charlie. She and Molly at number 8 have been lifelong friends as well as near-neighbours for the past 47 years. Her daughter 'Dot' lives in the Old Road.

7 Manor Road has been home to Winifred Taylor for the past 45 years. Her husband Fred worked at Yeoman's Garage from the time it first opened until his death in 1990.

Molly Wilson at **8 Manor Road** was born at Palace Cottage in 1920. Both she and Dolly Coldicott at number 6 attended Clifton school in the 1920s before Molly went 'into service' for a Martley family and later at what is now Clifton Court until war broke out when she went to work on the land. Her family had meanwhile moved to Resthaven near the New Inn. She and her husband were among the first residents in Manor Road.

Mark Butler at **9 Manor Road** is one of four Butler brothers living in the village, sons of Dave and Margaret at number 11 Manor Road. Builder Mark and his partner Caroline Chamberlain have lived at their present address since the birth of their nine-year-old daughter Amy.

10 Manor Road has been home for Tex and Margaret Powell for the past 34 years. The couple first met while Tex (a nickname that he has had since childhood) was serving in the Army at Norton Barracks in the 1960s. Margaret now works for Forest Fencing at Stanford Bridge but Tex has retired from his job with Hereford and Worcestershire County Council. Their two sons and two daughters now all live in neighbouring villages.

David Butler at **11 Manor Road** originally came to Clifton as the site foreman for Kenelm Close when it was being built 30 years ago and he and his wife Margaret have lived in Manor Road ever since. David now specialises in barn conversions. In 1999 Margaret took over as school caretaker from Peggy Hooper. One of their four sons, Darren, lives with them and provided the disco at the Lion Inn on New Year's Eve, celebrating his 29th birthday on New Year's Day. Their other sons, Kevin, Mark and Brian all live in the village.

David and Cathine Merry have been at **12 Manor Road** for 13 years. Cathine's parents live nearby at number 3 and the couple have three children, Louise (21), Corrine (19) and Craig (11). David works for Clarcon in Worcester while Cathine helps out with turkey-plucking and plum picking at Pitlands. She vividly remembers floodwater sweeping through the farm after the April downpour in 1999.

Edna Fletcher came to live in Clifton from Birmingham in 1969, moving into **13 Manor Road** as soon as it was completed. Her son John, now at Bury's Place, moved into the village shortly afterwards. Now at the age of 91, she spends most evenings with her neighbour Cissie Devereaux, usually playing Scrabble together, finishing with a glass of sherry, "but never on a Sunday," she insists. Becoming a great-grandmother in 1999 was, she says, a memorable moment.

Pensioner Angela Niblett at **14 Manor Road** continued her involvement with the Parochial Church Council and Church activities as well as the WI and the Clifton Gardeners in 1999, tenderly maintaining the two rosebeds at the top of Manor Road. She particularly recalls the St. Kenelm's Flower Festival and the re-hanging of the church bells. Angela moved to the village 12 years ago and her sister Elizabeth lives at Chapel House.

Angela Niblett

Joan and Roger Glanville

New Year's Day 2000 was a special day for Roger and Joan Glanville at **15 Manor Road** for they celebrated their diamond wedding anniversary. The couple met at Harper Adams Agricultural College before the war and married near Dover in 1940. For the next five years, Roger saw active service at Dunkirk and in North Africa before being captured and spending three years as a POW in Italy and Germany. In 1945 he escaped and eventually made his way behind the American army lines to be reunited with Joan for the first time in five years. Roger and Joan came to live in Clifton in 1979 after he retired from his job with the Ministry of Agriculture.

Mary Klein moved to **16 Manor Road** 18 years ago, having moved to number 18 in 1977 with her late husband. She has been an active member of the village community for many years and still runs what she calls her "small essential car!" Her daughter Elizabeth Rowe lives a few doors away at number 22.

17 Manor Road has been the home of Robin Yeomans since 1972. Robin, whose father Herbert Yeomans ran Yeomans Garage until 1986. Robin bought the adjoining property, **18 Manor Road** in 1998.

Dave and Samantha West moved into **19 Manor Road** in 1999.

Pam Banham came to live at **20 Manor Road** 14 years ago with her husband Alf who was the village postman for 27 years. Since his death two years ago, Pam has enjoyed many evenings playing crib at the New Inn, though more recently has found the late evenings too much for her years.

21 Manor Road is the first house that Stuart and Frances Miles have owned since moving six times in four years before coming to Clifton a year ago. 1999 saw the birth of their first child, Robert, in April; both he and Frances attend the Mother and Toddler group in the village. Husband Stuart, a New Zealander, is a lecturer in sports science at University College, Worcester. Both he and Frances are keen runners, walkers and cyclists and think Clifton is a "brilliant" place for such activity.

Elizabeth Rowe with two of her paintings

Artist Elizabeth Rowe at **22 Manor Road** now has a considerable reputation for the quality of her still life oil paintings of fruit and vegetables, many of which are bought by galleries. Although she has lived in Clifton for 20 years, she discovered her talent more recently and now finds that her work is in constant demand. Her son Nick now lives in Colorado.

Lewis and Winifred Cracknell came to live at **23 Manor Road** from Essex 24 years ago when Lewis was employed as a lecturer in accountancy. Lewis, now retired, is a former senior lecturer in accountancy at North London Polytechnic.

'Kit' Cox at **24 Manor Road** celebrated her 85th birthday in December 1999. Though born in Sheffield, Kit and her husband used to visit her neice, Diane Mann, at Pitlands until eventually they decided to move into the village altogether 20 years ago.

Next door at **25 Manor Road** lives Beryl Withington, mother of Penny Arkinstall at Knoll Cottage. Beryl was living in Warwickshire when her daughter and husband moved to Clifton, but soon followed herself. 1999 was particularly memorable for the arrival of her fourth great-grandchild, and celebrating her 80th birthday in December - an event she shared with near-neighbour Margaret Wragg who was 70 the same month.

At **27 Manor Road** Karl and Jenny Everard welcomed the arrival of their baby son Thomas in 1999. Karl is a self-employed agricultural technician and Jenny is now involved with the Clifton Toddler group.

Ray and Nicola Clark moved next door at **28 Manor Road** five years ago to be nearer their parents in Tenbury and think Clifton is a good place to bring up their children, Georgia (4) and Sophie (2), whose birthdays are only a week apart in January. The family added Jake, a black Labrador, in 1999.

Gwyneth Pardoe has lived at **29 Manor Road** for the past 15 years and insists she "wouldn't leave the village if I won the Lottery." In addition to being treasurer of the British Legion women's section, Gwyneth devoted time to caring for two elderly people in 1999. She proudly recalls receiving a commendation from King George VI during the war for her part in rescuing an airman from a burning plane.

Brian and Judy Richards moved into **30 Manor Road** when it was built in 1968. Brian runs a garden and farm machinery business, while Judy works for a florist's shop in Bromyard owned by Brenda Crump.

Richard Bedhall (right) with neighbours Manor Road

31 Manor Road was the home of Mabel Turner since the 1970s when she moved from Laburnham Cottage on the village green. She was one of the first women in the village to own and ride a motor cycle. (*Sadly, Mabel died on 4th January 2000*)

Richard Bedhall, a member of the team producing this book, moved into **32 Manor Road** at the end of 1999 having returned to Clifton after ten years lecturing at an agricultural college in Hampshire. The year also brought a change of career and he now works as an estate agent for Russell Baldwin & Bright in Tenbury Wells. He is a member of the St Kenelm's bell-ringers. His parents, Bob and Pauline Bedhall, live at Stone House in Pound Lane.

Vickie and Susie Walker at **33 Manor Road** say they will never forget the love and support shown to them by friends of all ages in the village after the death of their mother Shirley in April 1999. Both Vickie, a recruitment consultant, and her sister Susie, a nanny, have always lived in Clifton.

Graham and Yvonne Powell moved to **34 Manor Road** just over two years ago with their son Russell, aged 13, having previously lived in Riley Cottage (now occupied by the Holloways) in Pound Lane for three years after they married. Both Graham and Yvonne work at Kays in Worcester, though ill health kept Graham off work for several months in 1999.

Phil Probert

At **35 Manor Road** live one of Clifton's most senior couples, Phil and Jean Probert. Now in his 90s, Phil and his wife moved to Clifton from Shropshire to be near their daughter Heather Nuttall. Jean Probert is President of the local women's branch of the Royal British Legion.

Rob Holloway, a farm manager at Wichenford, has lived at **36 Manor Road** since 1983

Clifford and Dorothy Maund moved to **37 Manor Road** 15 years ago shortly after retiring from their respective jobs with the Health Service. Dorothy's nursing experience has enabled her to care for her husband after a major operation in 1999. She particularly cherishes her role as a chalice server at St. Kenelm's Church as well as her involvement with the Friendship Club and the weekly prayer group she attends. "We have found great fellowship here in Clifton," she adds.

At **38 Manor Road** Sharon Gannon spent time in 1999 renovating the bungalow she had occupied for nearly two years with her son Kieran. A sales officer supervisor, she has lived in Clifton for eight years.

Paul Fletcher at **39 Manor Road**, was looking forward to getting married in 2000 to his fiancée Sally-Ann Potter. Paul's brother lives in Hope Lane and his father John at Bury's Place.

For Jackie Gilbert at **40 Manor Road** the sudden death of her husband Ken in August 1999 was a devastating loss, but her commitment to community life in Clifton remained unshaken. She and Ken came to Manor Road in 1968 and their two daughters, Karen and Jane, were actually born in the bungalow. Jackie has worked with the Schoolhouse Under 5s Nursery group that she now leads for 21 years. "Some of the children I have seen grow up in the village are now married and have children of their own," she says. She is also a founding member of the Clifton Handbell Ringers and a member of the women's British Legion section.

41 Manor Road is the home of Peter and Margaret Wragg and their two young grandsons, Simon and Leigh, who came to live with them in October 1999. Since moving to Clifton four years ago, the couple have had to cope with the sudden death of their eldest son. "We have had such wonderful support from new friends and neighbours," they say. "We and our family have been made to feel so welcome."

Clifton's oldest resident at the turn of the millennium was 95-year-old Violet Devereaux, known to all her friends and neighbours as 'Cissie' because, she says, her brother was unable to say Violet so called her 'Sis'. Born in Harpley in 1904, she still vividly remembers having to walk long distances to and from school, even in the coldest weather and sometimes in deep snow. She and her late husband married at Harpley before moving to Kenilworth where they ran a nursery and shop until moving back to Clifton when they retired, coming to live at number **42 Manor Road** in 1980.

'Cissie' Devereaux,
Clifton's oldest resident,
with (right) Edna Fletcher

Kenelm Road

Built in 1964 on land that was previously a timber yard and allotments.

Bernard and Jennifer Pound have lived at **1 Kenelm Road** for 22 years. Both they and their daughter, Kate, are active members of the village community. Bernard, a Severn Trent Water manager, was elected Chairman of the Parish Council in 1999 and has been involved with the CPFA for many years, having been one of the people who developed and built the adventure playground on the playing field. Jenny helps with the local Brownies group, while daughter Kate is a member of the Guides as well as one of the Clifton bell-ringers.

Tony and Penny Watkins and their daughter Katy moved into **2 Kenelm Road** in the autumn of 1999.

Rudy and Kathleen Heilemann at **3 Kenelm Road** are partners in their own hairdressing business. The couple met while Rudy was serving in the US Air Force and married in the USA in 1959, celebrating their 40th wedding anniversary by returning there in April 1999. Kathleen was born in Martley and they have lived in Clifton for the past 25 years. Their two married daughters and five grand-children live locally.

Barbara Wilday and her mother, Vera

Next door at **Agape**, Richard and Barbara Wilday run a multi-media graphic design business from their home. Barbara is one of the three lay ministers in the parish, and is involved with both church and other parish activities as well as being co-opted to the Parish Council in 1999. Her mother, Vera Russell, lives nearby in Kenelm Close while daughter Georgiana and her husband are in Forge Meadows. Barbara remembers 1999 particularly as the year her niece, Deborah, to whom she was guardian, celebrated her 18th birthday thus fulfilling a promise to her late sister.

Cornerstones in Kenelm Road has been occupied by Terence and Jennifer Painter and their son Mark for three years.

Dave and Christine House spent their first ten years in Clifton in Kenelm Close before moving to **6 Kenelm Road** 18 years ago. Their daughter Joanne's wedding in July 1999 took place at St. Kenelm's church during the year. Christine, an office manager in Worcester, is secretary of the British Legion women's section and a member of the Clifton hand-bell ringers. Dave works as a claims investigator. Son John also lives with them.

Teachers David and Sue Warmington at **9 Kenelm Road** say they continue to be amazed at the peacefulness and tranquillity of the village, even after six years. Their daughters, Rosie and Ellie enjoy the Brownies and Rainbows as well as taking part in family services at St. Kenelm's church. Sue is also chairperson of the Scout and Guide hut.

10 Kenelm Road (*home of Gwen Westwood until her death in February 1999*).

Daphne Robson originally moved to Kenelm Close 25 years ago with her family, but now lives at **11 Kenelm Road** with her son Darren, a horticultural engineer. A trained therapist, Daphne is also a school superintendent in Clifton as well as a member of the St. Kenelm's choir, the women's branch of the British Legion and the Friendship Club.

At **12 Kenelm Road**, Donald and Ruth Roberts find life in semi-retirement in Clifton anything but dull. Ruth plays the organ when required at all four local churches and is involved with many other activities in connection with the church, including working with the group producing millennium kneelers. Both have lived in the village for the past 22 years and Donald keeps the churchyard grass cut behind St. Kenelm's church.

Kenelm Close

Built between 1970 and 1971.

At **1 Kenelm Close**, owned by Jenny Haywood of Midland Tree Care, is Karen Harris whose sister-in-law Lorraine Harris lives at 35 The Village. Her daughter Haley is aged five.

2 Kenelm Close is occupied by Christine Fletcher. Christine, a member of the group making the millennium church kneelers, has lived in the village for over 30 years, but remembers in 1999 making her way up Clifton hill in torrential rain in April when the road became a river of floodwater.

William and Edna Ashforth came to live at **3 Kenelm Close** 16 years ago to be nearer their daughter Christine next door at number 2. They were delighted with the arrival of their great-grand-daughter Emma Louise Fletcher in Hope Lane in 1999.

Vera Russell

Tony and Helen Thomas and their 14-year-old daughter Rachel moved into 4 **Kenelm Close** in 1999

Vera Russell came to Clifton eight years ago, moving to **5 Kenelm Close** in 1995 to be near her daughter, Barbara Wilday, in Kenelm Road. She particularly enjoyed singing Fauré's Requiem with the church choir in 1999.

Ann Jackson at **6 Kenelm Close** is the last remaining original resident in the close. Until her retirement at the end of 1998 she commuted to Stourport where she worked for the same firm as Mike Snelling.

Vera Heggie at **7 Kenelm Close** came to Clifton in 1972 when her late husband Donald was appointed vicar. "He couldn't believe his luck when the Bishop of Worcester offered him Clifton," she says. For four years, they lived at the old vicarage (now Burleigh Court) until moving next door when the present vicarage was built in 1976. When Donald died suddenly in 1978, followed shortly by Vera's mother, Vera moved into her mother's home where she has remained since. For nearly 20 years, until the beginning of 1999, Vera was Practice Administrator at the Knightwick and Clifton surgeries. Her two sons have moved away from the area and at the age of 76 she now enjoys a well-earned retirement.

Agricultural engineer Kevin Butler and partner Suzanne Harris have lived at **8 Kenelm Close** for five years. Suzanne works for National Power. Kevin's parents and brothers Mark and Darren live in Manor Road.

Geoffrey and Stephanie Milner at **9 Kenelm Close** decided to make Clifton their home after attending the Jazz Festival three years ago.

Jeff and Sue Pinson came to **10 Kenelm Close** from Malvern in 1972. A retired BT engineer, Jeff now offers to help local residents with TV aerial and reception problems as a hobby. More recently he has developed a static aerial for mobile phones in order to overcome the poor reception in the area.

Colin Watmore at **11 Kenelm Close** left the Royal Navy after 29 years service in 1999, became a fire brigade technician and a co-opted member of the Parish Council. With his son and wife Jan, a telephone receptionist, he has lived in Kenelm Close for 15 years.

Roger and Carolyn Wiggins and their son John have lived at **12 Kenelm Close** for 15 years. Roger is a site agent, Carolyn a call centre advisor while John is a technical college student.

Mike and Pat Snelling at **13 Kenelm Close** first came to Clifton in 1968 to live in Manor Road, moving to Clematis Cottage opposite the village shop ten years later. After moving to Tenbury for four years, they returned in 1985 to their present home. Mike, purchasing manager for a Stourport ceramics firm, is a churchwarden, bell-ringer and chorister at St. Kenelm's as well as being the church clock winder, a duty he performs religiously every week. Pat, a home care manager for Worcestershire social services, is training to become a lay reader. Both she and Mike are PCC members.

Pat and Mike Snelling

Royal Mail manager Rosemary Holloway and her daughter Kirsty live at **14 Kenelm Close**. Rosemary's family has lived in the Teme valley for several generations and she came to Kenelm Close in 1984. 12-year-old Kirsty is a member of the Clifton-upon-Teme Pony Club.

Dave and Sue Merrick moved into **16 Kenelm Close** at the end of 1999 with the rest of their family, Amelia (21), John (15) and Emily (14). Dave, a contracts supervisor, has lived in the village for most of his life and his mother lives nearby. Sue is a litigation and conveyancing assistant.

Tree surgeon Alan Butler has lived at **17 Kenelm Close** for 26 years. His son Steve, also a tree contractor, lives at Forge House opposite the Lion Inn.

Saxon Close

Nine houses and 30 bungalows built between 1967 and 1968 in a field that had five natural water springs. As a result, some of the buildings have suspended floors because of the height of the water table.

Saxon Close residents

At **1 Saxon Close**, Neil Parkinson looks back on 1999 as the year he started his own animal feeds business based at Cleobury Mortimer. Born at Homme Castle, he managed Ham Farm for 13 years where he was joined by his partner, Sally Edrop, former landlady of the Crown Inn at Martley. The couple have a 3-year-old son, Jack, and moved to Saxon Close two year ago.

David Yarnold has lived at The Limes, **2 Saxon Close** for nine years, after moving from the temporary home he occupied for a number of years in the Old Road. He and Brenda married in 1997 and Brenda's love of gardening has resulted in them winning the village garden award on more than one occasion. Sadly, 1999 was to see the demise of David's agricultural machinery business at the top of the Old Road, a victim of the depressed economic state of farming.

3 Saxon Close has been the home of Ross and Marina Dixon for 24 years, where they now live with daughter Rowena (21) and son Lewis (18) who works for Midland Tree Care. For Marina, a clinical nurse specialising in palliative care, 1999 was marked by the death of her father, Bill Richards, in August, who farmed at the Thrift in Pound Lane

Irene Bradley moved to **4 Saxon Close** in 1998 from Worcester, following the death of her husband. She now enjoys taking part in the Friendship Club and British Legion activities, having settled happily into village life.

Alice Bagshaw's most memorable moment in 1999 was watching the church bells being taken down in April, marvelling at the dust of decades and wondering how the bells had been lifted into the belfry centuries ago. Now retired, she continues to enjoy life in Clifton from her home at **5 Saxon Close** where she has lived for 15 years. "Few places have a pub like ours," she says. "Long may it survive."

Bob and Gillian Collins at **6 Saxon Close** came to Clifton 20 years ago and spent the first four years at Noak Farm before moving to their present home. Bob was born in 1936 in one of the three cottages that became Ham Bridge House at the bottom of Clifton Hill. One of their daughters, Julie, lives with them while her sister Lorna lives at 16 Forge Meadows.

The Goddard family at **7 Saxon Close** have a particular interest in country and wildlife activities in the area. Don Goddard is a wildlife consultant specialising in wetland ecology and entomology as well as being a member of the New Inn shoot for which his eldest daughter Hannah also beats. Don's wife Ann, a school's liaison officer at Hindlip College, is actively involved with the Clifton guides, brownies and rainbows as well as occasionally helping with the schoolhouse nursery. The Goddard household had a sizeable pet population at the end of 1999, including six guinea pigs, three hamsters and two ducks cared for by Hannah and her sister Jennifer.

At **8 Saxon Close** are Graham and Hazel Hickling and their four children, Gemma (11), Chrissie (9), David (7) and two-year-old Jules. Hazel's big moment in 1999 came when she staged a production of her own play, On The Edge at Malvern Theatre in March. Written and directed by her, it was based in part on Annette Carter's experiences in Romania the previous year. Composer, playwright and director, Hazel was a founding member of the Angel Theatre Company. She and her husband, a pensions manager, came to Clifton eight years ago.

Michael and Kate Shrubb moved into **9 Saxon Close** in 1987 after living for a year at Moorfields near Oxhall Farm. Kate is a director with the Maylite Trading Estate at Martley which her father Alan Wellings, who lives at Wyvern on the other side of Hope Lane, developed in the 1970s. Her husband Michael is a self-employed gardener, and the couple have two sons, Joseph (10) and Sebastian (4).

10 Saxon Close is occupied by Paul Tomkins.

Mark and Deborah Dennis have lived at **12 Saxon Close** for ten years. Mark's parents, Stan and Jean, live in the village and Mark, a builder, played football for Clifton Rovers for many years until April 1999 when the team disbanded. Deborah works for the Worcester Health Authority and the couple have two daughters, Georgina (5) and Ellen (4).

Graham and Karin Taylor at **14 Saxon Close** are among the few remaining original residents who moved in April 1968 when the houses were built. For 12 years the couple did the local milk and newspaper round, assisted by their daughters Louise and Denise. Graham now works for a Bromsgrove car dealership.

Ted and Pam Wojciechowski

Next door at **15 Saxon Close** live Tadeusz and Pamela-Jane Wojciechowski. Ted, as he is known to family and friends, came to Britain from Poland after the war. 1999 was a traumatic time for both when he was diagnosed as suffering from cancer. "Through prayer and the support of friends, we have tried to look to a positive future together and count ourselves very lucky," says Pam who values the friendship they have found in Clifton since moving to the village five years ago.

Pam became chairman of the village school governors and has involved herself in the school's activities, the Friends of Clifton School and the Schoolhouse Nursery. In addition, she has been a county magistrate for 18 years and is currently one of four deputy Chairmen of the South Worcestershire bench. Pam is also one of the team producing this book.

Janet Howes

At **16 Saxon Close** Janet Howes continued to enjoy her involvement with the Friendship Club, helping with the mini-market on the village green in September. "At my age, each new day is a bonus!" she says.

When Rachel Dixon came to live at **17 Saxon Close** two years ago with husband Roger, she was fulfilling a childhood dream to live in the village where she once spent her school holidays with her aunt and uncle who then lived at number 1 Saxon Close. Roger works as a land surveyor, while Rachel, whose mother Pam lives at number 15, is a training officer.

Roger and Rachel Dixon

Their next-door neighbours at **18 Saxon Close** are Richard Walker, a photocopier and facsimile machine service manager, and Karen Mandefield, a marketing communications executive. Richard helps with the production of the Church magazine.

Neville Jones and Claire Tissiman at **19 Saxon Close** originally lived elsewhere in the village before moving to their present address two years ago. For more than 14 years Neville was both farm manager and gamekeeper at Woodmanton, but now works as a carpenter, spending several weeks in 1999 rebuilding the dovecote at Burton Court, one of the oldest in the country. Claire is a local government officer with Worcestershire County Council and has a 13-year-old son David.

Andrew and Nina Haines moved to **20 Saxon Close** from Nottingham ten years ago. Nina, a nursery teacher, helps with the schoolhouse nursery in the village. The couple have two children, Cherish and Alexander, and say that Clifton is the 'ideal place to raise our children.'

At **21 Saxon Close** Grace Wright's year ended with a bad spell of pneumonia which saw her admitted to hospital just before Christmas. By New Year's day she was recovering and soon back in the home she has occupied for the past 22 years. Her toffee-making is much appreciated by the Friendship Club.

Joe Taylor

Joe and Jane Taylor at number **22** moved to Saxon Close eight years ago with their two sons John (13) and Richard (10) from Manor Road where they had lived since their marriage in 1982. Joe was born at the New Inn which his parents then kept. His grandparents, Joe and Annie Thompson, had previously kept the Lion Inn. The couple now run Taylor's Conservatory Care and several houses in the village now have one of Joe's conservatories. In September, the Taylors swapped houses with their neighbours, the Fletchers at number 24. Joe is a member of the team who produced this book.

Gerhard and Mary Schoenemann at **23 Saxon Close** were among the first residents of the close in 1969. Gerhard, a former Luftwaffe navigator, was captured two weeks before the end of the war at the age of 19 and interned in the PoW camp at Clifton. Instead of being repatriated in 1948, he stayed on and later married Mary in 1951. "Little did I realise when I was a prisoner in Clifton that I would end up buying a bungalow just a few yards from the prison camp I was in," said Gerhard.

Gerhard Schoenemann (seated centre) as a PoW in Clifton in the 1940s

Ray and Mavis Fletcher exchanged houses with Joe and Jane Taylor in 1999, moving from number 22 to **24 Saxon Close** so that Ray had more room to devote to his hobby, restoring a Hillman Imp. "It was a day to remember," he recalls. "It rained most of the morning, and wheelbarrows were put to good use for the occasion." The couple met while both were serving in the RAF and moved to Clifton from Derbyshire in 1998. Ray now works in the computer department at Kays in Worcester.

Mike and Peggy Pearson at **25 Saxon Close** were among the first residents to move into the close 31 years ago. Peggy assisted at the school and with the Guides for many years, but the couple's children have all left home and Mike and Peggy have continued to run their domestic appliance repair business in Worcester.

When Jean Benning first came to Clifton in 1968, she and her husband Harry lived at Cooks Cottage in Pound Lane. After Harry's death in 1979 she moved to **26 Saxon Close** to be nearer the village. She still maintains her involvement with the Friendship Club, having been one of the original committee members, and continues to sing with the St. Kenelm's Church choir. One of her twin daughters, Anne, lives with husband Neil Sparey in the village while sister Debbie has moved to Malvern.

Ernie Maudsley

27 Saxon Close was the home of Ernie and Irene Maudsley until first Irene died in August and then Ernie in December after a short illness. Since moving to Clifton in 1967, both were very active in village affairs; Irene with the school and church as well as being a founder-member of the Nomads, while Ernie served as a Parish Councillor for many years right up until his death as well as playing a prominent role in the management of the Village Hall as Chairman of the Trustees.

28 Saxon Close is the home of retired teacher Horace (or 'H' as he is generally known to friends and neighbours in Clifton) and Elaine Potter. The couple married three years ago following the death of H's first wife Edna in 1990. He was one of the first occupants of Saxon Close 35 years ago and in his time has been involved in choral singing locally as well as at one time helping with the football team and the scouts and cubs. 'H' also made the notice board in the village hall and the one in the centre of the village.

Michael and Mary Kipping moved to **29 Saxon Close** four years ago from Martley where they had lived for 19 years.

Derek and Janet Brooks have lived at **30 Saxon Close** for 24 years. Janet is a member of the local WI. Both their children have now moved away from the area.

Forge Meadows

The name reflects the origins of the site, once a grass field at the back of the blacksmith's yard belonging to the Haywood family. Work on the site commenced in 1990 with the last house being sold in 1996. Of the 23 houses, 11 are still occupied by the original purchasers.

Gavin and Janet McLaren have lived at **1 Forge Meadows** for three years with their daughter Jessica, now aged five, and latest addition, Steven, born in 1999. They have been in Clifton for eight years, having moved from number 6 Forge Meadows which they bought when it was first built in 1991. Jessica belongs to the Rainbows whilst other members of the family were involved throughout 1999 with various school activities, the Motorcycle Show, the Flower Festival, the May Day Show and the Music Festival

At **2 Forge Meadows**, Tania Morris is the most recent arrival, having moved to Clifton towards the end of 1999 when she came here to purchase her first house. Tania, a commissioning engineer, celebrated her 30th birthday in 1999 and is looking forward to getting involved in the village.

3 Forge Meadows belongs to Peter and Gail Darby who were living abroad in Lusaka, Zambia, at the end of 1999. Peter is an export manager for a farm produce company. The couple moved to Forge Meadows seven years ago and have two sons, Jack (8) and Mark (5) who have been attending the international school in Lusaka where their mother Gail also teaches. They still consider Clifton as home, however.

Philip and Lynne Asker have lived at **4 Forge Meadows** for nine years. Philip belongs to the Table Tennis Club, an exclusive group of enthusiasts who meet regularly during the winter months. Lynne is a former governor of the village school. Their daughter Sarah lives in Lime Cottage, one of the new houses on the opposite side of Pound Lane.

Emma Grace, a primary school teacher, and Les Woods, at **5 Forge Meadows**, are particularly attracted to the village for its walking opportunities and they use the footpaths often. Since they arrived in the village nearly three years ago, they haven't noticed too many changes other than their immediate neighbours moving in and out, but they expect the new housing development to change the village in future.

6 Forge Meadows was for sale at the end of 1999.

Roy Gwilliam has lived at **7 Forge Meadows** since the house was first built in July 1991. His daughter Shelby lives next door at number 6 although she plans to move shortly. Roy retired in 1999, but during the nine years he has been in the village he has noticed the building of new houses and the arrival of more new people.

Margaret Breakwell at **8 Forge Meadows** came to the Teme valley from the Black Country during the war to work as a 'Land Army' girl. After marrying a local man, the couple lived in one of the three cottages that now form Ham Bridge House, later moving to Woodmanton Lodge and Hope Cottage where she remained until 1991 when she moved to Forge Meadows. She maintains a particular interest in Clifton's history.

Georgiana Baxter has lived at **9 Forge Meadows** with her husband Steve for six years, having originally moved to Kenelm Road with her parents, Richard and Barbara Wilday, 12 years ago. Her grandmother, Vera Russell, also lives in Kenelm Close. Georgiana is a graphic designer whilst Steve is a product manager with Forest Fencing.

Liz Peel, together with her daughter Erica, occupies **10 Forge Meadows**. Liz moved to the village nine years ago but has lived in the area for 25 years. She has been actively involved as Clerk to the Parish Council and has helped with the Village Hall renovation projects. She is looking forward to joining the gym at Martley Sports Hall which is due to open in 2000.

Kathleen Knight moved to **11 Forge Meadows** as its first occupant in July 1992. Kathleen's daughter Ann and grand-daughter Sheila live at New House Farm in Pound Lane. Now aged 80, Kathleen enjoys taking part in the local sewing group.

Jeremy and Susan Haywood built their own house at **12 Forge Meadows** six years ago. Jeremy, one of the four Haywood brothers, has lived in the village all his life and has seen how new houses and new people have helped to keep the village alive.

Parish Clerk, Liz Peel

14 Forge Meadows next door was built by Jeremy's brother, Nick Haywood who now lives at Oak House adjoining the Post Office.

Julia Haywood with baby Maia

Matthew Haywood (brother of Jeremy and Tom at numbers 12 and 15b and Nick at Oak House) lives with his wife Julia and daughter Maia at **15a Forge Meadows**. The plot at number 15 was originally planned for one large house but in due course was divided to build two smaller houses. A major event for Matthew and Julia in May 1999 was the birth of their daughter Maia in May, while Matthew was able to help with taking down and re-hanging the church bells in St Kenelm's church after they had been restored. He was also involved with the rebuilding of the church bell tower at Harpley church. With brothers Tom and Nick, Matthew took over the Haywood family building business from his father Phil in 1999. He enjoys visiting the Lion Inn and playing football for Martley.

Tom and Linda Haywood moved into **15b Forge Meadows** in 1998. For Tom, a regular member of the Clifton Rovers football team until it disbanded, 1999 was memorable as the year he became a director of the family building firm of G. Haywood & Sons, following his father Phil's retirement. Linda, whose mother Jenny runs Midland Tree Care in Hope Lane, works for the Hereford Chamber of Commerce.

Ian and Lorna Davies have lived at **16 Forge Meadows** since March 1996, but they have long connections with the village as both their families have occupied Noak Farm at different times. Ian spent his early childhood there while for Lorna it was her teenage years with her parents, Bob and Gillian Collins in Saxon Close. Ian's parents, Harry and Sylvia Davis also live with them as well as their daughter Gemma. Lorna is an active member of the school support group, being events secretary, and was involved with the Christmas bazaar and the May Fayre in 1999. For Ian and Lorna, the memorable event of 1999 was their 15th wedding anniversary.

Ian and Gill Prest are the original occupiers of plot 17, now known as **Anvil House**. They have two children, Adam and Katie, and particularly enjoyed the Millennium celebrations at the end of 1999.

Gerald and Lyn Emery are the original occupants of **18 Forge Meadows**, moving from Hagley (as have a number of village residents). They were introduced to the village by Philip and Lynne Asker who live at number 4. Gerald and Lyn are both retired and keen walkers (they provided Derek Leavey with a number of walks for his book). In 1999 they started up the Clifton Wanderers, a small walking group. They also enjoy gardening and are active members of the Clifton Gardener's Club, helping to prepare the 1999 entry for the Flower Festival at the Church. Gerald enjoys cabinet making as a hobby and has made all the furniture for their house while Lyn is an artist. They memorably joined the computer age in 1999 with the purchase of a computer and connection to the Internet.

Don MacLean

Next door at **19 Forge Meadows**, Don and Doreen MacLean are the original occupants, and were actually involved in the design of their house. Both are involved in a number of activities in the village, including the walking group and the Bowls Club, where they have taken part in numerous matches. Doreen works part time at the Post Office and is also an active committee member of WI. They recognise that there have been changes in the village in recent years: "we have lost a butcher's shop but have gained a vet and four new bungalows".

Nick and Vicky Harper live with their daughter at **Heligan House**, originally number 20. They are very involved with the village, particularly the Toddler Group, events at the school, the Lion Inn and the Clifton Music Festival. Nick lived in the village from 1968 when his parents built Little Paddock in the Old Road, but left with Vicky to move to Tenbury Wells in 1994 only to return with his family in 1999. There are currently four generations of Harpers living in Clifton at present: Bessie Harper (Nick's grandmother) at Cedar Cottage, Pound Lane, and Nick's mother Kate at The Anchorage. Heligan House takes its name from 'The Lost Garden of Heligan" (19th Century Gardens in Cornwall).

Harry Kent moved to Clifton and **21 Forge Meadows** four years ago from North Wales. Lancashire born and bred and proud of his lifetime working in the textile industry, Harry is now retired and moved to be near one of his sons who lives in Great Witley.

Barry and Jan Pearce have lived at **22 Forge Meadows** since the house was built in 1993, having moved from Worcester. Barry is a member of the CPFA while Jan helps run the Friendship Club. "Although there have not been many changes since we moved to the village, the sense of community spirit is stronger than ever," they say.

Austin and Tracey Birks have occupied **23 Forge Meadows** since it was built in December 1993. Austin works as Commercial Manager for a bus company, and their daughter Abigail started to attend Clifton school in 1999 when they became involved in a number of activities at the school and pre school group including various fundraising events. Austin and Tracey pay occasional visits to the two pubs in the village and enjoy living in Clifton.

Pound Lane (Whitbourne Road)

Pound Lane is named after the village pound, located where the Recreation ground is today, used to keep stray livestock. The original pound in Clifton was near the Lion Inn. The land now occupied by Blue Shot and the four new cottages was the site of a POW camp during the 1939-1945 war.

Among the last people to move into Clifton in 1999 were Michael and Yvonne O'Callaghan at **Maple Cottage**, one of four new houses to be built next to the school. Both were born in Redditch where they have lived for the past 49 years. They especially enjoy walking with their dogs in the area.

Peter and Jean Knight plan to enjoy retirement at **Chestnut Cottage** since moving into the village at the beginning of 1999. In addition to getting their new garden organised, they have planted a flower tub in Pound Lane which they intend to maintain.

Bessie Harper, mother-in-law of Kate Harper, returned to Clifton in 1999, moving into **Cedar Cottage**, having lived in the village for several years during the 1970s when her son Ken and his family lived at Little Paddock in the Old Road. She celebrated her 89th birthday in December.

Lime Cottage is home to Sarah Smith and her daughters, Becky and Katie who attend the school nearby. Sarah's parents, Phil and Lynne Asker, who live across the road in Forge Meadows, used to have a holiday home in Saxon Close and she recalls coming unwillingly to stay in Clifton at the age of ten but has since changed her opinion and now thinks "it's a smashing place to bring up children."

At **Blue Shot**, adjoining, George Bewley now builds racing cars as a hobby after retiring from the motor-racing gearbox business he ran from his premises since moving to Clifton 16 years ago. His passion is building and racing cars for hill climbs, competing at venues throughout Western Europe.

CLIFTON-ON-TEME YOUTH HOSTEL, TEME VALLEY, WORCESTERSHIRE

The Youth Hostel in the 1950s, now Blue Shot

The PoW camp on this site during the 2nd World War housed mainly Italian and some German prisoners. The inmates were 'trustees' allowed out to work on local farms but kept to a curfew. The prisoners would give sultanas, sweets and money to local children, some of whom remember an Italian officer in full inform, complete with ceremonial sword and polished riding boots, strutting up and down inside the large wire fence that surrounded the camp. After the war, the camp became a Youth Hostel until the 1950s when it was bought by Johnny Williams who named it Blue Shot because "buying it was a shot out of the blue".

Douglas and Pauline Ratcliffe lived for many years at Bury's Place before moving to **Mount Pleasant** on the southern edge of the village, 25 years ago. Douglas has variously been the District Councillor for 16 years, Clerk to the Parish Council for 12 years and, more recently, Chairman of the Parish Council until 1999. In addition, he is a member of the PCC, Village Hall committee and the local British Legion branch. Not surprisingly, at the age of 82 he feels it is time to let others take over some of the duties he has performed for so long. The village has changed tremendously," he says. "When I first came here 28 years ago, it was a very rural community, with many people still employed as farm labourers. I was one of only two residents who commuted to work each day." Pauline Ratcliffe is famed for the marmalade she makes every year in the kitchen of their 17th century house. In 1999 she made 400lbs of which was sold to raise money for the church.

Flint House, the home of Roger and Christina Atkinson and sons Sam (9) and Ben (6), is approached along the drive leading down to Hill Farm.

Brian and Lisa Butler have lived at **The Knoll Bungalow** on the Hill Farm estate for six years, though Brian has lived in the village most of his life. A self-employed tree-surgeon until February 1999, he has since been employed by Herefordshire County Council. His parents and three brothers all live in the village. He and Lisa have two young sons, Jack (5) and James (3).

The Knoll Cottage, below Knoll Bungalow, has been occupied by company director Jerry Arkinstall and his wife Penny for 18 years after its conversion from a farm cottage. Their elder daughter Julia married local builder Matthew Haywood in 1998 who now live in Forge Meadows.

David and Bea Beasley at **The Knoll Barn** were abroad at the end of 1999.

Martyn and Sally Lidsey came to **Hill Farm** ten years ago from Banbury and have extensively renovated and restored the imposing Queen Anne farm house and outbuildings. The farm's 150 acres are put to grass, while Sally trains horses for dressage. An international dressage judge and former Olympic team selector, she has three horses of her own. Hill Farm was previously occupied by the Richards family and later by John Lyon.

Sally and Martyn Lidsey with O'Leander at Hill Farm

Oxhall Cottage, on the right along Pound Lane, past the turning to Hill Farm, has been occupied by teacher Gwynne Hignall for ten years.

At the **Cottage of Content**, Richard and Vanessa Stephens celebrated the christening of their daughter Anna in June 1999. The couple have came to Clifton ten years ago and Richard is in the Royal Navy.

Stuart and Gay Jackson and their daughters, Josie and Holly, moved to **The Salt Box** in 1999 from Buckinghamshire. The house was originally built about 1690 and its name is thought to derive from having been occupied by a local salt merchant. Between 1900 and 1960 it was occupied by the Shepherd family. Mrs Shepherd, known locally as 'Granny Shepherd' is said to have had 64 relatives living in the area. After her death, the building was unoccupied for several years and eventually had a demolition order put on it, but was saved by Pauline and Tony Peacock who owned it until 1999, extensively renovating and extending it before selling it to the Jacksons..

Farmers Peter and José Pheysey at **Upper House** recall the Gardens Open Day in 1999 with amusement because Peter was asked to bring his vintage John Deere tractor to the Church Farm field used for car parking to tow a car out of the pond where the lady driver looking for a 'cool' place to park had left it! Peter was a member of the team that removed the church bells from St. Kenelm's and helped to clean and paint the bell frame. Both are active members of several village organisations.

Peter and José Pheysey

Farmer Dennis Churchill at **Moorfields**, next to Oxhall Farm, farms at Stanford Bridge.

Derek and Dorothy Leavey came to **Cooks Cottage** 20 years ago with their three daughters. Despite being nearly a mile from the village, Dorothy says modestly: "We wanted to be part of village life and have been involved in many local activities." In fact, she is the St. Kenelms church organist and choir-mistress, having recently conducted the augmented choir in a performance of Fauré's Requiem; a parish councillor; led the sewing group making the millennium altar-rail kneeler in 1999, is involved with the WI and teaches music. As the parish footpaths officer, Derek led the team assisting with publication of the first parish footpath guide, Walks Around Clifton upon Teme, sponsored by the Countryside Commission and the county council. Their daughter, Susannah, was married in 1999. Susannah's sister Laura is a chef, and eldest daughter, Claire a freelance journalist, and her baby daughter Gabriel live with them. Claire Leavey was editing Classic Bike Guide when she suggested having a Classic Motorcycle Show in the village. With Derek and Dorothy's help, the first show was held in 1996, opened by the Bishop of Hereford, and has since become an annual village event. In 1999, it attracted more than 90 entries along with the Rev. Lionel Fanthorpe of Channel 4 fame to open it.

At **Oxhall Farm** Geoff and Jenny Farmer remember both the extremely wet weather in 1999 and watching the fireworks over Worcester on New Year's Eve. Geoff and his son Neil farm in partnership, with over 400 north country mule ewes, Suffolk rams and about 700 lambs, either sold for slaughter or kept for breeding, in addition to growing barley, wheat, beans and potatoes and grass for the sheep and for hay. The Farmer family have farmed in the area for over 100 years, and Geoff, Jenny and Neil have been at Oxhall Farm since 1969, having added considerably to the original acreage. The farmhouse itself was built in 1977 by Phil Haywood. Geoff and Neil are members of a local shoot and Jenny is clerk to the Clifton school governors, having been the infant class teacher between 1962 and 1990.

Peter and Ann MacBride (left) with Jenny and Geoff Farmer and son Neil

Peter and Ann MacBryde have lived at **Oxhall**, the original farmhouse below Oxhall Farm, for 30 years and, although now retired, both are active members of the Tennis Club and Bowling Club. Ann is also the joint leader and treasurer of the Friendship Club, having given up her part-time role as receptionist at the Clifton surgery in 1999.

2 Riley Cottage, has been home to Nick and Sarah Bradley and their daughter Georgina for eleven years. Nick, a building contractor, has lived in Clifton all his life. His parents live at Broadlands in the Old Road. Sarah was expecting her second child at the beginning of 2000.

Leslie and Diana Holloway celebrated their 40th wedding anniversary at **1 Riley Cottage** in July 1999 where they have lived for 13 years, now in retirement.

New House Farm is farmed by mother and daughter, Ann and Sheila Jones. The 140 acre farm dates back to the 17th century and was originally part of the Whitbourne Hall estate. In 1999, they had 280 ewes, 21 cows and nearly 40 followers as well as several acres of oats and barley. Ann's mother Kathleen lives in Forge Meadows. The water supply to New House Farm and other nearby properties is provided by a special water-powered pump installed in 1956 requiring no other power source to operate it continuously.

Sheila and Ann Jones at New House Farm

Eric Delahay farms 120 acres of accommodation land at **Gorse Hill** ajoining Newhouse Farm. Eric originally came to live at Oxhall Farm in 1933 but has since moved to Wichenford.

The Stone House, a renovated 300 year old stone building with many of its original features, has been the home of retired civil engineer Bob Bedhall and his wife Pauline for 24 years. Between them, they are involved with the British Legion, the Bowling Club, Friendship Club and the WI as well as the church choir and fabric committee.

Mulberry Barn, Thrift Court has been occupied by John and Gillian Widdowson, their son Daniel and niece Caroline for four years. One of the highlights of 1999 for them was when their horse came second in his class at Burwarton show.

Chris and Ann Cale at **2 Thrift Court** enjoyed celebrating the New Year on the village green in Clifton. Since moving to their present home six years ago, Chris has become vice-chairman of the Clifton school governors while Ann is an active member of the WI.

Sales director Nick Rendle has lived at **Tryfan Barn, Thrift Court** with his daughters Lucy and Joanne for five years. Nick is a member of the Clifton Tennis Club.

4 Thrift Court is home to head teacher Maggie Goodwin, her daughter Kate and grandson Thomas, born in September 1999.

Steven and Caroline Leigh moved into **5 Thrift Court** in January 1999 from Solihull where Steven is the Borough Architect. Caroline is studying for an Open University degree.

Thrift House was the original Thrift Farm house, occupied by Bill Richards and his family, until Robert and Penny Stead bought it 16 years ago. Both Robert, an audiologist, and Penny, a part-time nurse at Ronkswood, are members of Clifton Tennis Club. One of their sons, Alex, works as a graphic designer from home, while brother Guy pursues a musical career in London.

Thrift Farm Bungalow was occupied by Bill Richards until his death in August 1999 at the age of 73, and his son Maurice who works with the Haywood brothers building business.

Bill Richards (seated) with sons Maurice and Harvey, Diane, Lydia and Verity pictured shortly before Bill's death in August 1999

At **Lower Thrift Farm** Maurice's brother Harvey Richards continues the family farming business that has existed since the Richards family came to the parish in 1910. The farm's 160 acres accommodate a flock of 500 breeding ewes as well as several acres of cereals and growing cider apples for a Storridge cider producer. The farmhouse itself was built in 1990, but Harvey was born at what is now Thrift House. Harvey's wife Diane is the company secretary for the National Beef Association as well as being a governor of Clifton school attended by daughters Lydia (8) and Verity (6).

Hope Lane *(Originally called Maile Street)*

Corner Cottage at the top of Hope Lane probably dates back to the 16th century. Its present owner, barrister Peter Anthony, extensively rebuilt one end of the timber-framed building before moving in four years ago.

Postman Reuben Saunders outside Corner Cottage c1910

Mike and Hilary Bloomer moved into **The Beeches** when it was built 13 years ago. Hilary is a member of the PCC and St. Kenelm's choir as well as a sales and consumer researcher. Their daughters now live in the London area but enjoy occasional visits to Clifton.

Wyvern has been the home of Alan and Rita Wellings for ten years. It was originally named after a local radio station by the previous owner.

Surgery

Desi Green MBE

Built in 1976 after relocating from the old Vicarage (now Burleigh Court) where the doctors' surgery had previously been located. A branch of the Knightwick practice of Drs Tony Collis, Andrew Bywater and Anne Lewis, the Clifton surgery operates on Monday and Friday mornings.

Attached to the Surgery is Community Nursing Sister Desi Green MBE. Desi was awarded her MBE in the New Year's Honours. A popular figure in the village, she has cared for many elderly, ill and disabled residents in recent years.

Village Hall

Built by public subscription in 1921 as a Parish Memorial Hall, the Village Hall still displays the memorial to local residents who served or were killed during the First World War. The hall became a registered charity in the 1960s when extensive renovation work was urgently needed. New toilets, kitchen and reception facilities were added and, more recently, improvements have been made to the car park, roof and heating with the aid of a grant from the District Council and funds raised locally. A Village Hall management committee administers the building.

Cousins Glynne and Margaret Richards moved to **Hope End** three years ago after Glynne finally retired from farming at Waters Farm, Upper Sapey where he had been for 60 years and was a founder member of Upper Sapey Cricket Club.

Bob Barnes at **1 Hope Lane** was born at Woodmanton Lodge below the New Inn, celebrating his 64th birthday in 1999. He has lived in his present house, one of six built in 1922, for 42 years and describes himself as a semi-retired painter and decorator, a trade he has carried on for most of his life in the village. In the 1960s and 1970s, he played football for Clifton Rovers.

Bob Barnes

Colin and Janet Morley and their three children have lived at **2 Hope Lane** for three years. Colin's parents keep the New Inn where he runs the New Inn shoot as well as managing his own building business, helped by his eldest son Lee who is also training to be an agricultural engineer. Daughter Sarah (14) is at school in Martley while four-year-old Matthew started school at Clifton in September 1999.

Mark and Alison Fletcher at **3 Hope Lane** celebrated the birth of their daughter Emma in 1999. Mark is general manager of Clifton Engineering, the business started by his father John who lives at Bury's Place, as well as being a governor of Clifton school. Alison, a primary school teacher, has taught at the school and more recently has become involved with the mother and toddler group as well as a member of the tennis club.

Gwen Daniels on her 76th birthday in June 1999

At **4 Hope Lane** live 'Beau' and Carole Jauncey and daughter Katie. 'Beau' is a self-employed gardener and tree-feller, while Carole produces painted glass craftwork at home. She gained her yellow belt at kick-boxing in 1999.

Robert and Petra Brookes on their wedding day, May 1999

Robert and Petra Brookes celebrated their marriage at the end of May 1999, having lived at **5 Hope Lane** for nearly five years. Petra's son Connor (7) attends Clifton school while his two-year-old brother Matthew goes to the nursery.

Gwen Daniels has lived at **6 Hope Lane** for 43 years, but after the death of her first husband, she eventually remarried to Douglas, a retired gunsmith. Gwen celebrated her 76th birthday in June 1999.

Jenny Haywood at **Hollywell** runs Midland Tree Care, a business started in 1977 when she was then living with her family at number 1 Kenelm Close. She has lived in Clifton for 27 years, and moved to Hollywell four years ago when it was first built, and now manages the business with the help of her son Christopher and several local tree surgeons including John Davies at Noak Farm, Steve Butler and Lewis Dixon. "We do anything to do with trees except plant them," says Jenny who undertakes contract work for the MEB and the railway network. She also has several acres of arable land in the parish which she share farms with her nephew. Her youngest daughter Linda lives in Forge Meadows, and her son Christopher was married locally in April 1999.

Tom Richards

Tom and Joan Richards built **Highfield House**, along the lane leading to Lower Sapey, in 1968 after buying their 400 acre farm from what was formerly Hope Farm. The couple had previously lived at the Hill Farm which had been in Tom's family since 1910 and where Tom himself was born in 1931. Tom now manages the farm with his son Philip, producing wheat, oats, barley, peas, potatoes and oil seed rape as well as sheep. Tom is a past chairman of Clifton Parish Council, and Joan is a founder member of the WI as well as being a member of the PCC and Pony Club committee.

Yarnton House Farm just past Highfield House farm has been the home of retired farmer Mary Douglas-Osborn for 20 years. A keen gardener, she enjoyed having her garden terrace re-slabbed in York stone in 1999.

The Hope, an early 18th century building, is now the home of Shane and Candy Connolly. The farm's 70 acres are mostly farmed by their neighbour, Tom Richards, but Candy has planted several acres of trees which she nurtures with great care. It has been in Candy's family, the Dennistons, for over 30 years. Candy, a freelance music teacher specialising in Carnatic (South Indian) music hosted a visit by her music guru from Madras in July, taking him to Whitbourne Primary School for a demonstration concert. Husband Shane continued his work as a professional floral decorator in London, where his clients have included 10 Downing Street and the Royal Academy of Arts. Candy's sister, Sue Everitt and husband Allen recently moved back to live in Lower Sapey, while brother Nick and family are at Sapey Court Cottage.

Candy and Shane outside The Hope

Coppice Cottage has been occupied by teachers Ray and Sue Ellson for ten years.

Old St. Bartholomew's Church, Lower Sapey

Friends of Old St. Bartholomew's Church

Old Saint Bartholomew's church at Lower Sapey is a rare example of an almost unchanged rustic Norman church (there is mention of a priest there in the Domesday Book), modified from time to time over the centuries. Evidence of an even earlier church on the site has recently been discovered. The present building was replaced by a new church at Harpley in 1876. Restoration work by volunteers has been supported by the setting up of a Trust - The Friends of Old St. Bartholomew's.

Mike and Pat Prosser bought **Old Church House** in 1989 when it was still known as Old Church Farm, first renovating one of the 17th century barns to enable them and their two sons, Nicholas and Timothy move in the following year. Since then, they have begun restoring both the granary and the cider mill, preserving the latter as a working feature. The ancient pool beside the house has been drained, cleaned out and coupled to a series of waterfalls to bring water in and out. At the same time, Pat began to resurrect the nearby ancient church and its churchyard, a process that took five years to complete, saw the creation of The Friends of Old St. Bartholomew's Church and resulted in the Churches Conservation Trust taking the building on. The main house remains empty still because of major structural work that is required to make it habitable. Some of the window frames date from before 1540 while its great 17th century inglenook is a later addition.

Allen and Sue Everitt and their son Tom (12) finally moved into **Sapey Pitchard**, a barn conversion near the remains of Sapey Court, in April 1999 having lived on site for a year. Allen is a retired Lloyds broker and Sue is a GP whose practice is at Upton-on-Severn. Her sister Candy lives at The Hope while brother Nick and his wife Jen have Sapey Court Cottage.

Paradise, a local beauty spot at Lower Sapey

Computer programmer Jeremy Sumner and his wife Melinda, a physiotherapist, have lived at **Hope Barn Cottage** for 11 years and admit to being "quite reclusive." 1999 saw the completion of their timber built garage by local builder Graham Gibbs, a project that began ten years ago.

Behind them is **Hope Barn Farm**, converted in 1990 and now occupied by Ian and Sarah Thirlwell and their two children. Ian is a builder and Sarah a classroom assistant at Brockhampton school.

James and Molly Loach at Hollands Mill as it is today and (right) in 1932

There has been a mill on the site of **Hollands Mill** since the 14th century. The present house, probably dating back to the 18th century, has been the home of its occupants, James and Molly Loach, for 16 years though they have owned it much longer. The couple moved from Birmingham when James retired from the engineering business he ran and today the 34-acre smallholding they farm has 60 ewes, 13 bullocks as well as poultry.

Woody' Walker with Michael and Cathie at Hope Mill

When Terry and 'Woody' Walker moved to **Hope Mill** in 1976 it was completely derelict, without water or electricity. Both worked hard for several years to refurbish the property, during which time their son Michael and daughter Cathie arrived. Woody teaches at the Chantry High School in Martley while Terry is now self-employed as a hydraulic engineer. The 20 feet diameter water wheel is at the back of the half-timbered mill house next to Sapey brook, and the original mill workings and grindstones are still there. From the kitchen window is a magnificent view of the waterfall. At the end of 1999 the family were preparing to move, having sold Hope Mill.

Old Road

The end of 1999 saw the closure of **David Yarnold Machinery** at the top of the Old Road, the agricultural machinery sales and servicing business that its founder, David Yarnold, had steadily built up over 22 years, having started on his own from the nearby Green Garage in 1977 after 20 years with Midland Shires Farmers Ltd. At its height, the business employed 14 people, moving to the existing site in 1984, and provided a service to farmers and landowners over a 25-mile radius, including the sale of quad bikes. Its eventual demise in December was, according to David Yarnold himself, the inevitable consequence of the depressed state of the farming industry. "The present government has left farmers to fend for themselves, and things have been gradually getting worse for the last three or four years," he says.

Pippa Balch on Honey, with Chris outside Copperfields

Chris Balch moved to **Copperfields** with his first wife, Jane, in 1978. The house had previously belonged to the Farmer family at Oxhall Farm in Pound Lane. After Jane's death in 1990, he married Pippa, a hospital theatre sister in Worcester. In addition to her involvement with the Parochial Church Council and the WI in the village, Pippa's main interest is riding. In 1999 she won through to the final of the Horse of the Year Show at Wembley on "Honey" her 22-year-old Welsh cob mare.

Malvern View next to Copperfields dates back to 1837 and is now occupied by David and Pat Bench who bought it in 1967. Since gaining her art degree at Birmingham eight years ago, Pat has worked as an expressionist painter in oil on paper, choosing social and family issues as her subject, though she admits that her paintings are "not comfortable".

Sisters Margaret Spratt and Dorothy Oldham came to live at **Westcott Close**, the bungalow opposite Copperfields, nine years ago.

1 Old Road has been the home of Alf and Lillian Williams and their son Stephen for 16 years. Lillian spent the first 15 years of her life with her family at Cooks Cottage in Pound Land, attending school in Clifton.

Graham Gibbs with sons Richard (left) and Carl (right)

Donald and Mary Lloyd came to live at **2 Old Road** 31 years ago. Their son Simon has since married and moved away.

3 Old Road is occupied by Dot Coldicott, whose mother lives in Manor Road.

4 Old Road is the headquarters of G.C. Gibbs, the building business that Graham and his two eldest sons, Richard and Carl, have operated since Graham started up on his own 14 years ago. Graham and Janet married in 1975, living briefly at Forge House before moving to their present home. Their youngest son Grant is an assistant manager in Worcester. (*Graham died suddenly in February 2000*)

Bob Mitchell has lived at **5 Old Road** for 62 years. He spent his first five years in the village in one of the three cottages that stood where Jill Yeomans now lives next to Yeomans Garage.

At **6 Old Road** live Stuart Bullock and his father Bill, now retired. Their family have lived in Clifton for over 30 years, though sadly Stuart's mother Margaret, a familiar figure in the village, died in July.

Bill Bullock

Bert and Pat Bradley were the first occupants of **Broadlands** when they moved in 30 years ago. Now in his 70s, Bert has lived in the district all his life where he still runs his plant hire business. After the death of his first wife Joan, he married Pat and their 23-year-old twins, Emma and Edward still live with them. A past-chairman and present member of the Parish Council, Bert is also the parish tree warden and on the village hall committee. Pat is a member of the church choir, Clifton Handbell Ringers and the guides.

Bert Bradley (right) with sons Nick (centre) and Andrew

At **Windrush** where they have lived for nearly 12 years, retired deputy head-teachers Michael and Frances Towey are now enjoying their home and garden in its beautiful location overlooking the Teme valley. Both enjoy classical music concerts in the area as well as attending the Hay-on-Wye and Cheltenham Festivals. 1999 saw Mike pass AS level German while Frances completed a long woodcarving course under the tuition of a master carver. Keen gardeners, they opened their garden for the Open Gardens Day in the summer. "We have also been delighted to find that many overgrown public footpaths are now open with signposts and stiles, enabling us to walk the area and enjoy to the full the beautiful views all round," says Mike. "We are blessed in these days to be able to enjoy a night sky without the infringement of urban lighting - a beautiful experience to be treasured."

Alan Burns moved to **Little Paddock** ten years ago with his wife Brenda who devoted much of her time to her garden until her death in October 1998. The family, including Brenda's daughter and two sons, organised a celebration of her life in March 1999. "She made the garden a place of beauty and peace," says Alan, a retired BT executive who is currently treasurer of the Clifton Gardeners, maintaining the enthusiasm shown by his wife. The house had previously belonged to the Harper family.

Clifton Court, the home of Angela Timmis and her son William, was built in 1937. Angela has lived there since 1969. Her husband Paul, who died in 1990, founded Forest Fencing at Stanford Bridge.

The Collett family at **Warwick Ridge** have become well and truly integrated into village life since their arrival 14 years ago. Roy, Managing Director of an engineering business, is a member of the St. Kenelms Church fabric committee, while his wife Trish is a church warden, training to be a Lay Reader, choir member and President of the Clifton Women's Institute as well as teaching part-time in Worcester. Their daughter Charlotte at Leeds University recently became a national jujitsu silver medallist while son Mitchell is a former head boy of Worcester Royal Grammar School.

Ben and Brenda Pearson came to live in **The Cottage** above the New Inn 14 years ago. Brenda's lifelong love of horses led to her taking in and fostering two donkeys from a donkey sanctuary when she eventually decided to give up riding. The donkeys are a familiar sight at St. Kenelm's Church, attending on Palm Sunday and the 'Pets' service, though snow and ice prevented their appearance for the Christmas nativity in 1999 however. Although she is known as 'the donkey lady', Brenda is an active church member, responsible for cleaning the church brass as well as singing in the choir and helping at coffee mornings.

Brenda Pearson, the 'donkey lady'

The **New Inn** dates back several centuries. For many years it was known as Shortlands, serving cider and ale to anyone who stopped by on their way to and from the village. The 1881 census records that it was kept by 70-year-old widow Elizabeth Griffiths who farmed the 12 acres of land that went with it. Today's landlord and landlady are Lawson and Janet Morley. Lawson's parents, Cyril and Jessie, took over the New Inn in 1964 after moving from the Admiral Rodney Inn at Berrow Green where Lawson himself was born. While Janet's pulling pints behind the bar, Lawson occupies himself rearing sheep on the adjoining land. Their son Colin and his family now live in Hope Lane.

Janet Morley, Nicky Thomas, Peggy Hooper, and Angie Griffiths behind the bar at the New Inn

Resthaven, one of a pair of cottages by the New Inn, has been the home of Terence and Hazel Lucy for 30 years. Their daughter Claire, now aged 28, married an American and lives in Chicago, while their son Adam lives in Bristol since graduating from Bristol University.

Bob and Heather Davis moved to **Woodmanton Lodge** at the bottom of the Old Road nearly 12 years ago and 1999 was a particularly memorable year for them. Their daughter Amanda Jane married her Canadian fiancé at Shelsley Beauchamp in May, they celebrated their own Ruby Wedding the following month and, as project co-ordinator for the restoration of the church bells at St. Kenelms, Bob was able to see the project successfully completed. In addition to being a member of the bell-ringing team, he is also branch secretary of the local Royal British Legion and a member of the Clifton Bowling Club.

John and Sue Delahay have lived at **Gatley** overlooking Pitlands for 15 years. John, a company consultant who sold the Bromyard business he started 38 years ago in 1999, is a member of Clifton Bowling Club, while Sue is a member of the Tennis Club. The building was originally two cottages and was previously occupied by Martyn and Bunty Crump before they moved to Church House Farm. Gatley is recorded in the Domesday book as being a holding of nine acres.

John and Sue Delahay

Clifton Hill

Clifton Engineering 2000

Clifton Engineering moved to the 'green garage' premises at the top of the Old Road in 1993. The business manufactures patio heaters and components for gas appliances, with 14 employees managed by Mark Fletcher whose father John runs the parent company, Ambi-Rad. The original building was constructed in 1922 for George Burnham's bus company. At the time, the journey to Worcester by bus took about one hour. The service operated every day except on Thursday and Sunday. Goods and bicycles were often carried on a roof rack.

Burnham's buses c1930

At the **The Highlands** next door live the Stephenson family. At the end of 1999, father Sid was about to give up the day-to-day management of the Teme Driving School he started ten years ago to become a full-time county road safety officer with special responsibility for driver education. His wife Pat works part-time in the village shop as well as helping out at the schoolhouse nursery for the past 11 years. The couple celebrated their silver wedding anniversary in August. Their house, shared with daughter Jessica (17) and son William (12), was built in the 1950s.

Cockshot Cottage, further down the hill on the left was once part of the Woodmanton estate and has been Keith and Sylvia Jaffrey's home for 31 years. Keith, an insurance underwriter, started his own business during 1999. By December Sylvia, a freelance copy editor, was nearing the end of a three-year project editing the Oxford Bible Commentary, having recently completed editing the Oxford Companion to Christian Thought. Both Keith and Sylvia belong to an informal Christian fellowship group in the parish. Keith sings with the Worcester Festival Choral Society.

Part of **Woodmanton Manor** dates back to the 13th century when it belonged to the De Wysham family and was surrounded by a moat, remains of which can still be seen today. John Crouch bought it in 1563 and it remained with the family for over 300 years. The present house, a plain brick mansion, was built in 1829 and occupied by local farmer Richard Depper. It has changed hands several times since; more recently Gordon and Wendy Yardley came to live there in 1966 and in due course diversified from farming; Wendy started a successful art gallery and Gordon indulged his passion for Jaguar sports cars by operating a classic car business. In 1999 Woodmanton was sold to Raymond and Shoana Blin who arrived with their nine-year-old daughter Francesca from Scotland in April. It now accommodates the Kennox Stud, and the Blins have two stallions at stud there in addition to several mares and young stock.

Ayngstree, approached along the drive that leads past Woodmanton Manor, is the home of Ted and Pat Farrell. The present building is a former farmhouse built around 1830 on the site of a much older building dating back to the 13th century (mentioned in 1215 as having 28 acres) on the old Saxon footpath leading from Clifton to Tedney. The name Ayngstree is thought to be a corruption of the Norman French word 'anestie' meaning 'path through the wood'. Ted and Pat came to Ayngstree from the Potteries 30 years ago, restoring the farmhouse and outbuildings and preserving a fine stone cider apple mill, oast and hop drying room. Ted is now Reader Emeritus at St. Kenelm's church, having been licensed to preach and take services since 1959, but has also devoted his energies to the British Legion and the PCC for many years, while Pat was WRVS leader of the Friendship Club for ten years and is a former President of the WI. They celebrated their golden wedding in November 1999.

Ted and Pat Farrell at Ayngstree

Their daughter, Maureen, is married to Ian Fox and the couple have lived next door at **Ayngstree Cottage** for 25 years. 1999 saw Ian, a dealer development manager, and Maureen, a teacher, planning the wedding of their daughter, Alice, due to take place at St. Kenelm's church on 22nd July 2000, the same date and church as their marriage in 1972.

The Wain House, occupied by Raymond and Patricia Pratt for 12 years was originally used to house the wagons at Ayngstree farm.

Roger and Dee Ward at **Dale End Farm**, approached along the drive that leads below Woodmanton, both qualified for the England clay pigeon shooting team in 1999 and competed in the home international event. The couple, who have lived at Dale End for 16 years, previously competed in the Great Britain team, Dee winning the Clay Pigeon World Cup in 1994 while Roger was a Veteran Silver Medal winner in the European Championships in 1998. Roger has been a consultant radiologist in Worcester since 1973.

Chris and Heather Hurley moved to **Palace Cottage**, halfway up Clifton Hill, from Lancashire in 1998 and both have become involved in village activities. Heather, a part time lecturer at Worcester College of Technology, is involved with the W.I. (she recently became joint vice-chair) and Clifton Gardeners who organise the Open Gardens Day each summer. Chris, a senior bank executive until he took early retirement in 1999, was instrumental in obtaining funding for the Millennium Book Project and recently took on the role of Treasurer of the Tennis Club. They were intrigued with the name of their cottage and eventually came across a copy of a 1908 Clifton-upon-Teme parish magazine which suggested that the cottage became known as The Palace because of a previous tenant named King. They also discovered that it had been a grocery store for a time in the early 1900s. Chris and Heather particularly enjoy the views from their cottage and the changing seasons.

Heather and Chris Hurley outside Palace Cottage

Teachers Mike and Jo Pedersen reckon that Clifton is the most friendly place they have ever lived in since moving to **Oaklands** above Pitlands Farm nearly three years ago with daughters Sara, a trainee accountant, and Charlotte, a university student. The house itself had previously been called 'The Bungalow', though local people referred to it as 'the pavilion' because it resembled a tea planters' bungalow, and the original timber building built around 1900. The Pedersens have a framed indenture for the land, however, dated 1773. Mike himself had run a smallholding in Wales for several years before training to be a Welsh Presbyterian minister, interrupting that to become a teacher instead before moving to Clifton.

Pitlands Farm c1925

Pitlands Farm has been in the Mann family since 1927 when Sydney and Edith Mann, parents of the present owner John and his wife Diane, bought it just before their marriage in January the following year. The couple had four daughters in addition to their son John, two of whom - Doreen and Jean - still live in Clifton. Sydney had been a market gardener and Edith a waggoner in charge of an eight team timber carriage, but it was the 17 acres of fruit that attracted them to Pitlands. There was no electricity, and every drop of water had to be carried from a well 100 yards from the house that was still in use until the late 1970s. The fruit was taken to Knightwick and Newnham Bridge railway stations for transportation to markets throughout the country, as well as to Worcester market.

John Mann took over the 25 acre farm in 1963 when his parents retired to live in Hallow. He gradually built up the laying poultry flock to 12,000 birds, and the pig herd to 120 sows, employing three full-time workers. In time, however, the pig and poultry industry declined and the Pitlands farm business suffered similarly. John married Diane in 1974 and the couple had two children, Heather and Ian. By this time, pig-farming had ended at Pitlands and the Manns have since concentrated on fruit farming, rearing turkeys for Christmas and over-ready chickens. In due course, they converted the empty pig-man's bungalow into holiday accommodation and now have three self-catering properties which they let in addition to offering bed and breakfast at the farmhouse.

John and Diane Mann at Pitlands

Their most vivid memory is of the severe winter of 1980/81 when temperatures dropped as low as -28°C: "We were preparing the Christmas poultry when the snow and ice came and everything, including the turkeys, was frozen," John recalls. "What a nightmare! There was a brief thaw over Christmas and then the snow and ice came back with a vengeance. You don't realise how much a pig drinks until you have to carry every drop from the kitchen sink (the only water that wasn't frozen). With pig food supplies running out, friends brought the biggest tractor they had to try and pull our lorry up to the road so we could get out for supplies. It took two days of digging and pulling, and then when we finally reached the road, it looked like a bob-sleigh run. During lambing, we had a kitchen full of lambs that we were trying to warm and feed as the ewes were too cold to bother. I spent the coldest night of all with a sow in the farrowing crates, in a T-shirt, with a bowl of water that began to freeze as soon as it was in the shed, delivering a litter of 13 piglets - a process that went on all through the night! Thank goodness, we have never had another winter like that."

Noake Lodge further down Clifton Hill at the approach to Noak Farm has been the home of Colling and Marian Robson for the past 9 years, during which time they have carried out major restoration work on the building as a retirement project. Both are members of the Clifton Bowls team (Colling is Secretary of the Bowls Club as well as a member of the Clifton Playing Field Association), and they again participated in the Open Gardens weekend in the summer. Colling, a retired chartered engineer, was also actively involved in the restoration and re-hanging of the church bells during the year.

Marian and Colling Robson outside Noake Lodge

Neil Kirby at **Noak Farm** found 1999 a particularly difficult year, with crops and livestock fetching very low prices. The 170 acre farm that he farms has sheep, oats and wheat, part of the family business of A.M.Kirby (Martley) Ltd. The farm was first settled in the early 14th century when it was originally called Upper Holme. Neil occupies one half of the half-timbered farmhouse while Jim Davies, a retired farm worker, and his wife Maud live in the other half with their son John who works with Midland Tree Care.

The new building at **Clifton Park**, above Ham Farm was built in 1971 adjoining a 17th century cottage once known as The Ashes on what was once the route that led from the River Teme to Clifton. Paul and Sue Ridgway have lived there since 1994, though Sue originally came to Clifton in 1973, first at the Cottage of Content in Pound Lane and later in Harrisfield at the top of the hill climb above Shelsley Walsh. The house is shared with Paul's son Oliver and daughter Tory, and Sue's father Bill Kinchin who moved from Yorkshire three years ago. Paul's mother Betty lives in the cottage. Paul manages Ridgway Trading at Homme Castle while Sue is a sixth form tutor and former Head of Classics at the Alice Ottley School in Worcester

A water mill at The Ham is mentioned in the Domesday Survey. The existing **Ham Mill** house overlooking the River Teme, about half a mile downstream from Ham Bridge, was built in the early 1700s and at one time included a shop, bake oven and a malt house. Its present occupants, Clifford and Hazel Barnard, have lived there since they married in 1956. The original mill was demolished in 1900 although the millstones still lie on the site of the remaining building, bought by Cliff's parents Llewelyn and Kate Barnard in 1955. For many years until he retired in 1987, Cliff was employed as the Worcester City Parks Superintendent and today Ham Mill's grounds contain a remarkable collection of shrubs and trees planted up to 20 years ago. He and his wife spent 1999 maintaining their smallholding and garden, often taking their vegetables to the WI market in Bromyard. Of their three children, only their son Linden still lives at home. Cliff Barnard is a founder member of the Martley and District Horticultural Society and was President of the Clifton-on-Teme Britain in Bloom Committee. He is also the author of *The Tale of Two Villages*, a history of Clifton and Martley published in 1995.

Hazel and Cliff Barnard at Ham Mill

The new owner of **Ham Farm**, Stewart Mayfield, arrived with his wife Carole, and children David, Daniel and Gina from Norfolk in November 1999. The 400 acre farm overlooking the River Teme included 200 beef cattle, 750 ewes and 106 acres of cereals at the end of 1999 as well as 259 acres of grassland, much of it rented out. Ham Farm was originally part of the Manor of the Hamme and, like Homme Castle, is mentioned in the Domesday Survey.

Shelsley Road

Company directors Nick and Irene Stokes moved into **Harrisfield**, the cottage at the top of the Shelsley Walsh Hill Climb, in 1999. Not surprisingly, they have become members of the Midland Automobile Club that organises the four annual hill climb events at Shelsley. The half-timbered cottage lies within the parish of Clifton and was extensively restored and extended in the 1970s.

Shelsley Walsh Hill Climb

Along the road leading from Shelsley Walsh to Ham Bridge, James and Mandy Card live at **1 Castle Bungalows** with children Jodie, Stella and Christopher who all attend school in Clifton where Mandy helps with the younger pupils.

Next door, at **2 Castle Bungalows**, live Adrian and Tracey Wadley with their children Simon, Jessica and Jacob.

Homme Castle Barns, an office and industrial complex occupying converted barns adjoining Homme Castle. Development began in 1989.

Windmill Studios: (Paul Brazier and Rachel Bayliss) Manufacturers of fine bone china. 12 employees.

Ridgway Trading: (Paul Ridgway) Leather finishers and suppliers to the equestrian market. Four employees.

Real Dynamic Fitness: (Richard Dilworth) Health and fitness consultancy; specialists in lifestyle management. Three employees.

The Mayne Partnership: (Roger and Claire Mayne) Liability adjusters, handling claims for insurance companies. Three employees.

Milston Travers: (Anthony Milston) Financial services. Four employees.

Earlswood Estates: (Brenda Hughes) Commercial property rental and business management. Five employees.

C-Tech International: (Dennis and Gloria Dollings) Security marking and identification. Ten employees.

AIM Internet: (Mike and Sallie Raybone)

The earliest mention of a castle at **Homme Castle,** guarding the spot where the River Teme could be crossed by a ford, is in 1207 during the reign of King John. The original Homme Castle, a wooden structure surrounded on three sides by a moat, became the Manor of Homme Castle and was occupied for many years by the Jefferies family. During the Civil War of 1646, Cromwell's army laid siege to the building, bombarding it with huge cannon balls, causing considerable damage. Joyce Jefferies, who lived there at the time, died in 1650 and is buried in St. Kenelms Church in Clifton-on-Teme. A large half-timbered manor house replaced the building destroyed in the Civil War but this was later destroyed by fire in 1887, to be replaced by the present house now in possession of the Kirby family.

Homme Castle c1920

Homme Castle Farm has been farmed by Ian and Rosemary Kirby since 1970. The 268 acre farm included sheep, cereals and linseed in 1999. The couple have two children, Sarah (6) and Stuart (3). Ian's brother Neil farms the Noak Farm on Clifton Hill.

The Old Barn at Ham Bridge was converted by Leon and Monica Bell during the 1980s from a 15th century barn originally belonging to Ham Bridge House where they were then living. The couple bought the property in 1969.

Ham Bridge House has belonged to Francis Ducker since 1987. The building was originally a row of four cottages occupied by workers employed at Homme Castle and is known to date from the 13the century. A toll house was erected at the side of the road before even Ham Bridge was constructed in 1769. The road that now leads up the hill to Clifton was built in 1840.

Ham Bridge over the River Teme

Sapey Common Road

Ian and Sue Sparey

Ian and Susan Sparey live at **Otheridge Pool Cottage** opposite the remains of a cottage known as Custard Hall on the bend by the kennels. Ian now farms Steps Farm which he rents from the Brockhill Estate, having previously farmed at Stanford Bridge with his father and brother. In 1999, the farm's 256 acres were employed growing winter wheat, winter rye, oil seed rape, spring beans and sugar beet; although the yield was satisfactory, the prices were very poor. Both Ian and Susan were eagerly awaiting the arrival of twins at the beginning of 2000.

Kelly Stringfellow and Julian Brooke took over **Chandelle Boarding Kennels** and Cattery just before Christmas 1998 following an extensive search for the right property that would provide them with the boarding kennels they wanted having failed to find one they were happy to board their own dogs. As well as dog kennels and cattery, they offer a grooming service, sell pet supplies and will even board smaller pets such as rabbits and guinea pigs. "We've enjoyed our first year in Clifton immensely although we've been very busy," says Kelly. "We are still in the process of carrying out a major refurbishment of the kennels but we both look forward to many happy years in Clifton and hopefully, one day having time to become more involved with village life."

Kelly Stringfellow and Julian Brookes

John Yeomans (centre) with sons Robert and Andrew

Salford Court Farm is occupied by John and Dawn Yeomans and their sons Robert and Andrew. The 350 acre farm managed by John and his sons includes both cattle and sheep as well as growing wheat, barley, oats and rape. John's father, Jack, died in October 1999 at the age of 89.

Salford Court dates back to the 12th century. In 1290 Sir Henry Walsh, the landlord of Salford, obtained leave to have an oratory there and the chapel still forms part of the farmhouse. The Haywood family also occupied it for several generations. The present farmhouse is largely 18th century in origin, though it retains the large central hall which was the chapel and much 17th century panelling.

At **Salford House**, 82-year-old retired farm-worker Dennis Lippitt remembers the day when an RAF Blenheim bomber made a forced landing in a field near the farm in 1944 after losing its way in thick fog. Denny worked for Jack Yeomans for 60 years before retiring.

Brian and Sue Palmer moved to **Firs Cottage**, a mile out of the village, when they married in 1968. Sue was born in the Crown House when her grandmother, Maud Lewis kept a shop there; her brother Bernard lives in Manor Road, near their mother Mrs Violet Lewis.

Paul Botham came to live at **The Firs** with his parents 33 years ago, but is now the only occupant. Paul is an electrician with the MEB. His father John was chairman of the parish council before his death in 1983.

South Milestone Cottage has been home for David and Angela Roberts since 1993. Angela has close family ties to Witley Court, while her husband David comes from Wolverhampton and is employed as a coffee manufacturing manager for Nestlé UK.

David and Hazel Malley moved to **North Milestone Cottage** in 1997 from Nottingham. David is an operations manager for Severn Trent Water, and Hazel a member of the Clifton Gardeners and WI.

Sapey Common

Sapey Common begins at the county boundary between Worcestershire and Herefordshire.

The Camp House stands on the site of an old Roman camp, hence its name, and is now the home of Paul and Janet Smith and their four children: the youngest, Matthew is at Exeter University, while the other three are married. Their only daughter emigrated with her family to Australia in 1998. They bought the house in 1986. The previous occupants, the Milners, had lived there since 1914. It is said that Cromwell stored ammunition in the building before the Battle of Worcester, and local people still tell of the ghost of a Roman centurion seen guarding the entrance to the driveway.

At **Tally Ho**, the cottage next door to The Camp House, live Robert and Dawn Wattis and their sons Matthew (16) and Andrew (12). The family moved there in 1995 from Astley. Robert and Dawn run a business installing industrial cooling and chilling pipework as well as a domestic plumbing service, employing nine people.

Cliftonswood Lane

Holly Tree Cottage on the corner has been the home of Jim and Ethel Levins for 13 years. The 18th century building itself is in Herefordshire while the garden is in Worcestershire.

At **Cliftonswood Farm** Harry Brown farms sheep, cattle and cereals. The farm is named after Clifton Wood, an area of about 60 acres of ancient woodland that once provided honey for the villagers and food for their pigs. The farm itself lies on an old route from Woodbury Hill.

Linehill House opposite Cliftonswoods Farm was known as Ballards Farm until Simon and Patricia Lees-Milne moved there in 1983, but as it is marked as Linehill on Ordnance Survey maps they decided to revert to the original name. The house used to be a 17th century cider mill and was only partly converted when they bought it, although a Georgian wing had been added. Simon's family have lived in Worcestershire for several generations. Patricia is an active member of Sapey golf club, and was the Ladies' captain in 1999.

***

Sam the shire horse at home in Clifton

Graham Leake set up **Sam Shire Services Ltd**. at Sapey Common five years ago, manufacturing and recycling wooden pallets on a site vacated by a manhole cover manufacturer. He now employees 36 people and has enlarged the business to such an extent that it now also produces chipboard and horse bedding. With the help of Neil Sparey in 1999 he designed and built a machine to produce spacer blocks for pallets, using waste timber, the only one of its kind in the country. The business is named after Sam the shire horse owned by Graham's daughter Maggie.

Bluebell Cottage, opposite Rock Lane, was bought by Jim and Jackie Bell in 1999 to be near their daughter Angela and her family at The Brambles. The couple also bought the Baiting House inn at Upper Sapey, but they both spend a lot of time in Sydney, Australia, where Jim has several business ventures. The cottage itself was formerly known as the Pump House from the time local residents drew their water from there.

Rock Lane

Derek and Terry Johnson came to live at **Greens Cottage** in 1982 from county Clare in one of the most rural parts of Ireland. Their house was originally a woodsman's cottage on the Brockhill estate, lived in by several generations of the Green family until the 1960s; early 19th century maps show it marked as 'Mrs Green's Cottage'. Derek edits a plumbing and heating trade journal from home, assisted by Terry who recently retired from her post with the county education department.

Malcolm and Annette Carter have enlarged **Sunnyside Cottage** considerably since they bought it 18 years ago. The couple have three children: Emily, Edward and Sam. Annette spent two weeks in Romania in 1999 working with children in an orphanage. Malcolm has a passion for racing cars, having competed several times at Shelsley Walsh Hill Climb, and owns several vintage cars.

Glyn and Angela Miles moved into **The Brambles** two years ago with children Edan and Cari. Angela helps out with the Mother and Toddler group at Clifton school. In 1999 her parents, Jim and Jackie Bell, joined them in Rock Lane, buying Bluebell Cottage as well as the Baiting House inn at Upper Sapey.

Dave and Penny Davies live at **Hunters Ride**, having moved into their 17th century cottage in 1986. It had originally been extended some 30 years ago and they have enjoyed making a few changes of their own in both their garden and the building. Penny teaches textiles and is head of the Design & Technology department at Bishop Perowne High School in Worcester. Dave was Director and General Manager with GKN before retiring. He now works for his friend Paul Ridgeway at Ridgeway Leather in Shelsley.

Phil and Chris Bond moved to **Primrose Bank** in 1985 and have since extensively renovated their 18th century cottage. Phil runs a Land Rover and agricultural spares business as well as being a member of the North Bromyard parish council, while Chris is sales manager for a hygiene company. The couple have two daughters, Holly (7) and Pippa (3).

Rock Cottage is home to Dave and Denise Ball and their son Julian. Dave runs a garage in Stourport while Denise has a variety of jobs locally, including lunchtime supervisor at the Chantry School in Martley where Julian is a pupil.

Rock Lane leads down to Southstone Rock, once the site of a hermitage wher travelling monks would seek shelter in the caves.

South Stone Rock below Rock Lane c 1950

Park Lane

At **Park House** live Francis and Jennie Holmes and four of their five daughters (the eldest, Elizabeth got married in Antigua in 1999). Jennie is secretary to the St. Kenelm's Parochial Church Council, while husband Francis is a middle school teacher. Their daughters with them are Emma, Rachael, Rosalind - a member of the St Kenelm's Bell-ringers - and Isabel.

Print shop owners Chris and Gabrielle Buckland at **Arbour Lights** added a baby daughter, Victoria, to their family in September 1999 - a sister for Charlotte aged three.

Gary and Jo Williams at **2 Park Cottages** run their own Halesowen-based architectural ironmongery business. They have lived in Park Lane since 1996 and their daughter Bobbi was born in 1998. The couple organised a special Millennium party on the common on New Year's Eve for local residents, ending with a fireworks display at midnight.

Stuart and Lynsey Aston have lived at **Rose Cottage** since 1995. "We fell in love with the place and the area," says Lynsey. "It is quiet and also it helps having such good neighbours." The couple married in Montana in 1996, returning every year since. Stuart works for a cattle-breeding company as a breeding advisor, while Lynsey is with a Worcester firm that distributes industrial and leisure gas.

John and Mo Nicholson fell in love with their cottage, **4 Park Lane**, two years ago. "When we started to walk the local footpaths we couldn't believe the views and the unexpected natural beauty," they say. "We now wish we had lived here for the past 34 years instead of only two!"

Neil and Clare Sargent at **Fields Cottage** were delighted to learn at the end of 1999 that they were expecting their third child. They have lived there since 1986 and have a daughter, Jayne, and son Dominic. Neil works from home as an IT consultant.

Alan and Diane Yarnold and family

Alan and Diane Yarnold moved into **Valley View** when it was built in 1985. Alan farms with his father and brother at Criftens Farm nearby, the fourth generation of the Yarnold family to do so. The couple have two sons, Edward (10) and William (7).

At **Upper Warren**, Peter and Margaret Sparey have lived in semi-retirement for the past five years since moving from Mill Farm at Stanford Bridge where they had lived for 32 years and are still very much involved with. Their present home is a recent conversion of two adjoining barns.

Peter and Margaret Sparey

Mick and Betty Harper came to live in **Park Cottage** in 1970 when Mick was working for Yeomans Garage in Clifton. Their daughter Libby and grand-daughter Rosie, aged six, lives with them, while their son Steven is serving with the Army in Germany, having seen service in the Falklands, Bosnia and Northern Ireland with the Royal Army Ordnance Corps.

Mick and Betty Harper with Steven, Libby and Rosie

Jeff and Hilda Rogers and daughter Mandy moved to **Templewood House** in May 1999 having left Clifton in 1975. The family originally lived at the Crown House in the village where Hilda opened a tea room, serving tea and home-made cakes to visitors. Their daughter Lesley lives at Flint Cottage in Clifton.

Sapey Common Road

The Cottage is a listed 17th century building consisting of a timber frame and brick noggings. The cottage has had several owners since 1973 when it was sold by the Stanford Court estate. The present occupants, Joseph Hemingway and Judith Baker say: "every day here is momentous, but was crowned by the view from the common at midnight on New Year's Eve."

Don and May Saunders

Don and May Saunders have lived at Sapey Common for the past 53 years, 37 of them at **Benbows Cottage** on the bend opposite Criftens Farm, after moving from Park Cottage in Park Lane.

Freemans Cottage is the home of Barry and Jo Yarnold. Barry's father, Les Yarnold, lives at Criftens Farm.

Four generations of the Yarnold family have farmed **Criftens Farm** at Sapey Common. Leslie Yarnold, the resident farmer, does so with sons Alan and Barry. The 140 acre farm is now the only milk producer in the area, with a herd of 105 dairy cows and followers, as well as several acres of oats, barley and spring beans in 1999. Les's wife Norma died in December.

Thistledown Nursery, run Michael and Margaret Upton, was once Fox's Stores, the local shop at Sapay Common. Michael has lived there for 34 years, building up a business that provides tomatoes, cut flowers, bedding plants and hanging baskets. The couple married 12 years ago and Margaret runs workshops for anyone interested in creating their own hanging basket display.

The Carpenter family at Yearston Court

The Carpenter family have lived at **Yearston Court** since 1934 when Harry and Mary took over the tenancy. It had previously been farmed by the Holder family. The house itself is a large Edwardian three storey building, part of which once stood within a surrounding moat and is mentioned in the Domesday Book. The present occupants, Edward and Gwynneth Carpenter, married in 1967 and bought the farm from the Brockhill Estate. They have two children, Richard and Clare. From 1952 until the late 1980s, the family bred pedigree Herefords and Clun sheep, but now rear prime cattle, lambs and breeding ewes. The farm has employed one workman, Craig Bateman, for the past 17 years. The effect of the BSE crisis and EEC legislation has had a considerable impact on the business in recent years, however.

Gwynne and Jane Edwards moved to **Burton Court** in 1965 where they farm sheep and cereals on nearly 500 acres in partnership with their sons John and Alan. John lives in the farmhouse itself while Alan lives at Highview, a barn conversion. The dovecote at Burton Court dates back to the 12th century and was being restored by Neville Jones in 1999.

FARMING

by Jenny Farmer

The changing scene of the countryside around Clifton since the 2nd World War has been largely influenced by successive government policies.

During the war, the 'Dig for Victory' campaign saw many of the old pastures ploughed up to grow crops such as cereals, potatoes, sugar beet and mangolds for animal feed.

After the war mechanisation became the buzz-word in the 1950s, with most farms having at least one tractor and trailed implements. Some had a 'little grey Fergi' that could lift, pull and operate a variety of implements including a pick-up baler, modern plough and haymaking and harvesting equipment. The first combine harvesters and hop-picking machines also arrived in the locality.

The 1960s brought JCB diggers which greatly aided drainage schemes, hedge and orchard removal. The 'Small Farmer' scheme and the 'Amalgamation Scheme' and several others including the Common Agricultural Policy were introduced to help produce a reliable supply of cheap food. The resulting beef, butter and grain mountains in the 1980s were evidence of the success of such measures. As a result, quotas and other control schemes were brought in. Farming around Clifton had changed enormously in only a few decades.

By 1999, farming was in the doldrums - largely as a result of draconian measures introduced in the 1990s in response to BSE. Sheep and cattle farming, once profitable enterprises, suffered. The price of young breeding ewes fluctuated from over £100 to around £40. Cereal cultivation increased; 'diversification' and 'set-aside' were added to the farming vocabulary, barns were converted into dwellings at the Thrift Farm, Hill Farm and Steps Farm. Sugar beet and potatoes, widely cultivated in years past, were rarely grown.

Geoff and Neil Farmer harvesting 1999

The orchards that were a familiar sight around Clifton for much of the past century (a 'blossom trail' would draw visitors to the Teme valley in the Spring) have all but disappeared. Only Pitlands still has plums and apples, although a few cider orchards have recently been planted in the area. The last of the hop yards in the area was grubbed up at Homme Castle and the barns converted into business units. Several small farms amalgamated with their neighbours, others were split up and sold off and many local farmhouses sold off for private occupation.

Philip Richards sowing at Lower Sapey in 1999

A year on the farm: Oxhall Farm in 1999

Jenny, Geoff and Neil Farmer

The very wet weather was a great hindrance in 1999, making the rearing of lambs difficult. During the year, we had a flock of over 400 North Country Mule ewes and Suffolk rams. Lambing started in early February and March, producing some 700 lambs which were either sold for slaughter or the best ewe lambs sold for breeding. Lamb prices were at their lowest for 25 years for much of the year however.

The wet weather throughout April and into May made planting the Spring crops and potatoes very late which in turn led to the sheep shearing season starting later than at any time in 20 years of contracting.

The hay crop was very heavy, again probably due to the wet weather, which made for good growth and delayed cutting. The wheat crop yield was good and the weather reasonably dry while it was harvested. The straw was sold as 'standing straw' by auction which made good prices, as did the hay that was sold, although cereal prices were disappointing.

With more than four inches of rain in August and over five inches in September, including three inches in one day, the soil was too wet for planting. It never really dried out as more heavy rain fell in October. This prompted the purchase of a harrow/drill combination which was better for planting corn successfully in far from ideal conditions. Likewise, lifting the potato crop was also difficult though the yield was good; prices were poor however because of the large quantity of potatoes planted throughout the country, encouraged by last year's good prices.

CLIFTON-UPON-TEME FARMS - 1999/2000

At **Burton Court**, the Edwards family farm sheep, cattle and cereals.

Martyn and Robert Crump at **Church House Farm** have cereals, sheep and beef cattle as well as trading in hay and straw.

At **Cliftonswood Farm**, Harry Brown has sheep, cattle, cereals and root crops.

Criftens Farm, farmed by the Yarnold family, is the only dairy farm in the area.

Gorse Hill, farmed by Eric Delahay, has cereals and sheep.

Ham Farm changed hands in 1999 and the new owners, Stewart and Carole Mayfield, farm beef cattle, ewes, cereals and grass.

Tom and Philip Richards at **Highfields** off Hope Lane farm potatoes, cereals and sheep.

Hill Farm is now a grass farm with some cereals. Martyn and Sally Lidsey also keep a number of horses.

The Kirby family farm **Homme Castle** and **Noak Farm** where they grow cereals and rear sheep and beef cattle.

At **Lower Thrift Farm**, Harvey and Diane Richards' main enterprises are sheep, cereals and cider fruit.

Tony Kirby at Noak Farm

Ann and Sheila Jones at **New House Farm** have beef sucklers, sheep and cereals as well as a few hens.

At **Oxhall Farm**, Geoff and Neil Farmer have amalgamated several small farms and accommodation land. They farm sheep, cereals and a few potatoes.

John and Diane Mann at **Pitlands** grow fruit, rear chickens and turkeys, but have diversified into holiday accommodation and sell produce from their farm.

Salford Court, farmed by the Yeomans family, is more traditional, with beef cattle, sheep and cereals. It also has accommodation land away from the farm.

Cereals and sugar beet are grown at **Steps Farm** by Ian and Sue Sparey.

Woodmanton changed hands in 1999, and the new owners, Raymond and Shoana Blin, have several horses at stud on the farm as well as growing cereals.

Yearston Court and its accommodation land belonging to Edward and Gwynneth Carpenter is a livestock farm, with sheep and prime cattle.

Wildlife of Clifton-upon-Teme

By Dr. Don Goddard

Don Goddard

The Clifton area is fortunate in having a variety of semi-natural habitats that have not been too degraded by modern agricultural practices.

Otter

The River Teme is a relatively unpolluted river and this is reflected in the varied fauna and flora. Fish frequenting the river include Trout, Salmon, Chub, Bullhead and Stone Loach and Otters are said to be moving back into the area and have been reported from near Ham Bridge. The varying nature of the river with deep slow stretches, shallows, riffles and banks of fine sand and shingle provide a range of habitat for many scarce and rare invertebrates. These include the scarce River Saucer Bug Aphelocheirus aestivalis, an insect requiring very clean water. It never surfaces and stays submerged amongst stones in deep water. The only known county locality is at Ham Bridge. The Teme is also home to one of our rarer dragonflies the Club-tailed Dragonfly Gomphus vulgatissimus, so named because of the swollen end to its abdomen. This species also requires clean rivers for successful breeding.

On the negative side the banks of the Teme are in many places dominated by Himalayan Balsam. This is a tall, invasive foreign plant that has spread rapidly over many of Worcestershire's wetlands in the last two decades. When I first moved to Clifton there was none, now it can be seen dominating the bankside flora both up and downstream from Ham Bridge.

Apart from the River Teme and the many small streams that feed it as it passes through the parish, there are also large areas of broad-leaved woodland. Many of these woodlands are now largely unmanaged and harbour a rich diversity of insects, birds and small mammals as well as larger mammals like Foxes, Badgers and the introduced Muntjac Deer. A number of old orchards add to the diversity of the woodland habitat, perhaps the most noticeable feature here is the profusion of Mistletoe. Worcestershire along with Herefordshire are the national strongholds for this well known semi-parasitic plant. Sadly some of the old orchards have disappeared in the last decade.

Many ancient hedgerows criss-cross the parish. These are of great value for invertebrate life as well as providing nesting places for birds. Some of the older hedgerow trees (mainly oak and ash) provide roosting places for bats in their hollow interiors as well as supporting many species of scarce and local wood decay beetles. It is pleasing to see hedgerows still being traditionally managed in places by layering although the modern hedge cutters are all too evident as they are elsewhere in the country. Hedgerows provide vital wildlife corridors between woodlands, unimproved meadows, ponds and streams across the more intensively farmed land. Connectivity between habitats is vital for the overall well being of wildlife.

Hare

Much of the farmland in the parish is fairly intensively farmed, in common with that in most other lowland areas of the country. Modern varieties of Rye Grass and Clover are usually unattractive to most insects. However, there are still numerous unimproved and semi-improved areas of pasture. These areas of grassland support a diverse assemblage of insects providing food for many birds, such as the Grey Partridge. The unimproved pasture also provides a home for the Brown Hare. This is a mammal that is declining everywhere. In the pasture fields around Clifton one can almost guarantee to see a hare or two especially between November and March when the grass is shorter. In recent years these pasture habitats have been complemented by a considerable amount of 'set aside land' along field boundaries.

A keen observer may see a polecat crossing the road. This scarce mammal is slowly spreading eastwards from its stronghold in Wales and several are spotted each year.

Of course when discussing unimproved grassland one must not forget the many miles of roadside verges in the parish. These verges are often the only place the traveller will see large clumps of Snowdrops or large expanses of Cowslips and Cow Parsley. The latter plant is a vital nectar source for many insects. Nowadays grass verges are often the only places that the casual observer will see butterflies in any numbers. Species like Meadow Browns, Gatekeepers, Orange Tips and (the not so common any more) Common Blue used to be abundant in our meadows. Roadside verges have provided a valuable refuge as well as a linear corridor allowing movement between otherwise isolated islands of habitat.

Ponds are a rich wetland habitat supporting over two thirds of the nations wetland plants and animals. On a national basis field and village ponds are a diminishing resource. Many have been filled in or lost by neglect, due to changes in agricultural practices. Also, well meaning, but ill-informed improvements, such as overzealous desilting and the introduction of alien plants and excessive numbers of ducks and fish have ruined many village ponds. Clifton has three ponds in the village which are, fortunately, unimproved. One of them contains all three species of British newt, the Smooth Newt, the Palmate Newt and the Great Crested Newt. The Great Crested Newt is an internationally endangered species and has its world stronghold in Worcestershire, Gloucestershire and Herefordshire. This newt is fortunate in receiving full legal protection under the Wildlife and Countryside Act. There are only a few ponds in the fields surrounding the village probably due to the hilly nature of the surrounding countryside. This means we have to take especial care of our village ponds.

When I first moved to Clifton some twenty years ago I was struck by the unspoiled nature of the countryside and impressed by the wealth of wildlife compared to the arable desert I had moved from. Clifton upon Teme is still a haven for wildlife and long may it remain so.

Birds of Clifton-upon-Teme

By Keith Jaffrey

Keith Jaffrey

The variety of birds in any particular area is largely dictated by the habitat available and the food supplies that different species require. In the Clifton area there are four major habitats: the river Teme and its tributaries, woodland (mainly on the hillsides of the Teme valley), gardens and farmland - which sub-divides into pasture, arable and orchards. This diversity accounts for the large number of bird species that are currently found around here.

Birds also categorise into residents (R), summer visitors (S), winter visitors (W) and birds of passage (P).

The following is a list of bird types reported as seen in the parish in recent years.

WATER BIRDS
Grey Heron (R), Mute Swan (R), Canada Goose (R), Mallard (R), Wigeon (W), Teal (W), Coot (R), Moorhen (R), Kingfisher (R), Dipper (R), Grey Wagtail (R).

WADERS
Curlew (W), Lapwing (S).

GULLS
Lesser Black-backed Gull (P), Herring Gull (P), Black-headed Gull (P).

GAME BIRDS
Pheasant (R), Red-legged Partridge (R), Woodcock (R).

Buzzard

BIRDS OF PREY
Buzzard (R), Sparrowhawk (R), Kestrel (R), Hobby (S), Peregrine (P).

OWLS
Barn Owl (R), Little Owl (R), Tawny Owl (R).

PIGEONS
Woodpigeon (R), Stock Dove (S), Collared Dove (R), Turtle Dove (S).

SWIFTS, SWALLOWS
Swift (S), Swallow (S), House Martin (S), Sand Martin (S).

WOODPECKERS
Green Woodpecker (R), Great Spotted Woodpecker (R).

THRUSHES & ALLIES
Song Thrush (R), Mistle Thrush (R), Fieldfare (W), Redwing (W), Blackbird (R), Robin (R), Redstart (S), Black Redstart (W).

WARBLERS
Sedge Warbler (S), Reed Warbler (S), Whitethroat (S), Lesser Whitethroat (S), Garden Warbler (S), Blackcap (S), Willow Warbler (S), Chiffchaff (S), Wood Warbler (S), Grasshopper Warbler (S), Goldcrest (R), Spotted Flycatcher (S).

TITS
Long-tailed Tit (R), Coal Tit (R), Great Tit (R), Blue Tit (R), Marsh Tit (R).

CROWS
Jay(R), Magpie(R), Jackdaw (R), Rook (R), Carrion Crow (R), Raven (R).

Goldfinch

FINCHES
Chaffinch (R), Greenfinch (R), Goldfinch (R), Bullfinch (R), Linnet (S), Siskin (W), Yellowhammer (R), Crossbill (W).

MISCELLANEOUS
Pied Wagtail (R), Cuckoo (S), Skylark (R), Nuthatch (R), Tree Creeper (R), Starling (R), House Sparrow (R), Tree Sparrow (R), Wren (R), Dunnock (R),

There is no doubt that the numbers of birds of almost every species have diminished over the past thirty years. Lapwing, skylark and yellowhammer are few and far between following changes in farming practice. Visiting numbers of swallows, swifts and martins are less than before due to an increased use of pesticides killing off the flies on which they live. Even house sparrows and starlings have declined. There are, however, hopeful signs that enlightened attitudes towards the environment among those who have control over our countryside may stem the decline. Let's hope so, otherwise the wide diversity of our wildlife will not be in evidence a hundred years from now - let alone a thousand!

A bird's - eye view of Clifton-upon-Teme

Country Sports - Shooting

By Bernard Pound

Like much of the Teme Valley, the countryside around Clifton supports a significant level of the traditional country sport of shooting.

No longer the preserve of the well-off and privileged members of society, the sport is now enjoyed by a wide range of people, involving many local residents. On many days between September and the beginning of February, shooting parties meet at locations such as the New Inn, Salford Court, Burton Court and Ham Farm for a day of good company and good sport, whether as guns, pickers-up, beaters or stops.

To support the availability of quarry, which includes Pheasant, Partridge - both English (grey) and French (redleg) - and wild duck, a substantial rearing programme is undertaken. Once released to coverts, fields and pools, the ongoing husbandry of the birds also supports a wide range of other species, birds and mammals. These activities extend the period of interest for full and part-time gamekeepers and shoot helpers all year round.

New Inn shoot

Clifton-upon-Teme and Sapey Common

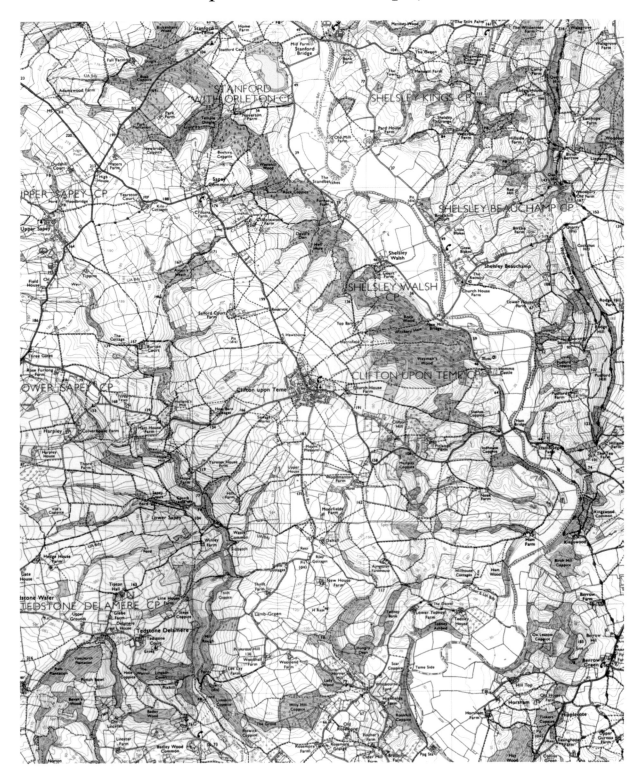

Clifton-upon-Teme in the 21st Century

The closing decades of the 20th century have been as changeable and difficult for Clifton-upon-Teme as they have for country dwellers elsewhere. Newcomers have occasionally been uneasy neighbours of traditional rural practices, sights, sounds and smells! House prices have escalated as Clifton came within commuting distance of larger towns and cities in the region. As a result, older residents and their families have been displaced by relatively well-off newcomers, a trend that has sometimes led to disagreement over issues concerning new developments. Agriculture has also seen profound changes in recent years. The plight of some farmers, hit by a series of crises and the ever-shifting demands of European agricultural policies has heightened a sense of isolation in the countryside as well as a feeling that the needs of those that live there are not understood by the urban majority or even the government.

Traditional rural sports and pastimes have also been under attack, most notably foxhunting. Although views differ on this issue, the threat to hunting is seen by many as a further attack on a way of life that is dependent on a sense of continuity. Other issues which have created problems include employment opportunities, especially for young people and the threat of closure of the village pub, school, post office, bus service or shops. The car, which has done so much to open up the countryside, has also taken trade away from local amenities as people pursue the choices offered by supermarkets and out-of-town shopping malls.

The list of problems continues to grow. But how is Clifton dealing with them?

In the course of compiling this book, many of the people who contributed information have commented on the changes that have taken place in the village. The increase in traffic and housing was particularly noticed, as was the arrival of younger families and the number of people commuting to work outside the area. Others remarked on the loss of amenities such as the butcher's shop, petrol pumps and greengrocer, but many welcomed the recreational facilities that have been introduced in recent years. More housing development in Hope Lane is promised and the school is flourishing, but what does the future hold for the present generation of children who are growing up in Clifton? Will they be able to find work in the area, and will they be able to afford the house prices if present increases continue?

Already there are signs of new employment being generated as modern technology is adopted in the area, with small business operating from the homes of self-employed residents and in converted agricultural buildings. Surely this trend will develop in future.

Fears that the village would become a haven for the elderly at the expense of young families have not materialised and recent new arrivals to the village have been readily integrated into the established but developing social fabric of Clifton.

Clearly there are many changes and problems which confront country life at the beginning of the new century, but if the picture that emerges from the pages of this book is any guide then Clifton is adapting well to them. What comes across is a portrait of a thriving and well-integrated community in a village still blessed with tranquil and beautiful landscapes in a working countryside where it is a joy to live, work and play and raise the next generation of children.

*Millennium Tree
on the village
green, 2000*

Births, Baptisms, Marriages and Deaths 1999

BIRTHS

January	Thomas EVERARD, 27 Manor Road
February	Emma Louise FLETCHER, 3 Hope Lane
April	Robert William MILLS, 21 Manor Road
May	Maia HAYWOOD, 15a Forge Meadows
August	Thomas GOODWIN, 4 Thrift Court, Pound Lane
December	Peter William BULLOCK, 2 Manor Road

BAPTISMS

6 June	Anna Elizabeth STEPHENS, Cottage of Content, Pound Lane
15 August	Emma Louise FLETCHER, 3 Hope Lane

MARRIAGES

22 May	Amanda Jane DAVIS (Woodmanton Lodge, Old Road) to David Christopher MILLS
29 May	Robert BROOKES to Petra WADLEY (5 Hope Lane)
10 July	Joanne Karen HOUSE (6 Kenelm Road) to Richard Christian COLES

DEATHS

Gwen Westwood (1915 - February 1999)
Born in Warrington, Gwen met her husband Gladwin at Birmingham University and married him in Cape Town the day after she arrived there. After taking a writing course, Gwen started to write children's books and later, Mills & Boons romantic novels. The couple moved to Kenelm Road, Clifton in 1978.

Shirley Walker (1941 - April 1999)
Born in Manchester, Shirley and her husband Mike moved to Saxon Close in Clifton in 1975 with daughters Vickie and Susie, before Shirley moved to Manor Road eleven years later.

Richard Roberts (1918 - May 1999)
Known to most of his friends as Dick, he was born at Corner Cottage in Clifton where he went to school and later worked as a carpenter with his father and later with Phil Haywood's father before joining the Lloyd Loom furniture factory in Martley. He married Florence and the couple had two children, one of whom, Rose Bethell, lives in Manor Road.

Margaret Bullock (1931 - July 1999)
A familiar figure in Clifton, Margaret Bullock lived in one of the Council houses in the Old Road for 38 years with her husband Bill whom she met while she was in the army. The couple married in Worcester 45 years ago and had eight children.

'Bill' Richards (1926 - August 1999)
Bill was born at the Hill Farm, one of 12 children of Lewis and Lillian Richards. After his father's death, when he was aged nine, he farmed The Hill with his brothers. He married Sheila Jones and eventually took over Thrift Farm where he remained until his death, though in later years his health declined following a stroke in 1992.

Irene Maudsley (1926 - August 1999)
Irene's early life was spent in the Manchester area. She met Ernie during the war when he was serving with the Royal Navy and the couple married in 1948. It was Ernie's employment with the Beecham Group that brought the Maudsleys with their son Clive to Clifton where Irene was one of the founder members of the Nomads as well as helping at the school.

Ken Gilbert (1936 - August 1999)
Born in Worcester, Ken left school to work in the printing trade, later re-training to become a nurse, first at Powick and later in Nottingham where he met and married Jackie. After Ken moved back to work at Powick hospital, they moved to Manor Road in Clifton in 1968. The couple had three children.

Aileen Moore (1907 - September 1999)
Aileen was born in Birmingham, the daughter of a German father and Gloucestershire mother. From an early age, she showed great promise as a pianist and, after studying at the Birmingham School of Music, became a professional accompanist. She and her husband Jack farmed near Chaddesley Corbett before the war, eventually moving to Clifton in 1976.

Jack Yeomans (1910 - October 1999)
Born in Herefordshire, Jack and his brother Herbert moved to Homme Castle with their father in 1927. He took the tenancy of Salford Court Farm in Clifton, in 1936 and married Olive Jones from Stepps Farm the following year, eventually buying Salford in 1944 where he soon gained a reputation for his great knowledge of livestock.

Ernie Maudsley (1927 - December 1999)
Born in Manchester, Ernie came to live in Saxon Close, Clifton with Irene in 1967 when he was appointed Area Sales Manager for the Beecham Group. During his time in the village, he served on the Parish Council, Village Hall Trustees, Royal British Legion, Football Club as well as a variety of other activities.

Kate Bakewell (1913 - December 1999)
Kate spent her childhood in Blackburn before moving to Banbury and later, during the war years, to Worcestershire where she served in the Land Army. She and her husband James built a house in Great Witley, but after his death she moved to Kenelm Close in Clifton in 1995.